THE ORIGINAL POOH TREASURY

THE

WINNIE-THE-POOH
STORYBOOK
TREASURY

A. A. MILNE

Illustrations by Ernest H. Shepard

CONTENTS
PAGE 1

Piglet Meets a Heffalump   9

A House is Built at Pooh Corner for Eeyore   39

Tiggers Don't Climb Trees   69

Winnie-the-Pooh and Some Bees   99

Eeyore Has a Birthday   129

Piglet is Entirely Surrounded by Water   159

CONTENTS
PAGE 2

An Expotition to the North Pole   189

Pooh Goes Visiting and   219
Pooh and Piglet Nearly Catch a Woozle

Christopher Robin Gives Pooh a Party   249

Pooh Invents a New Game   279

Kanga and Baby Roo Come to the Forest   309

Tigger Comes to the Forest and Has Breakfast   339

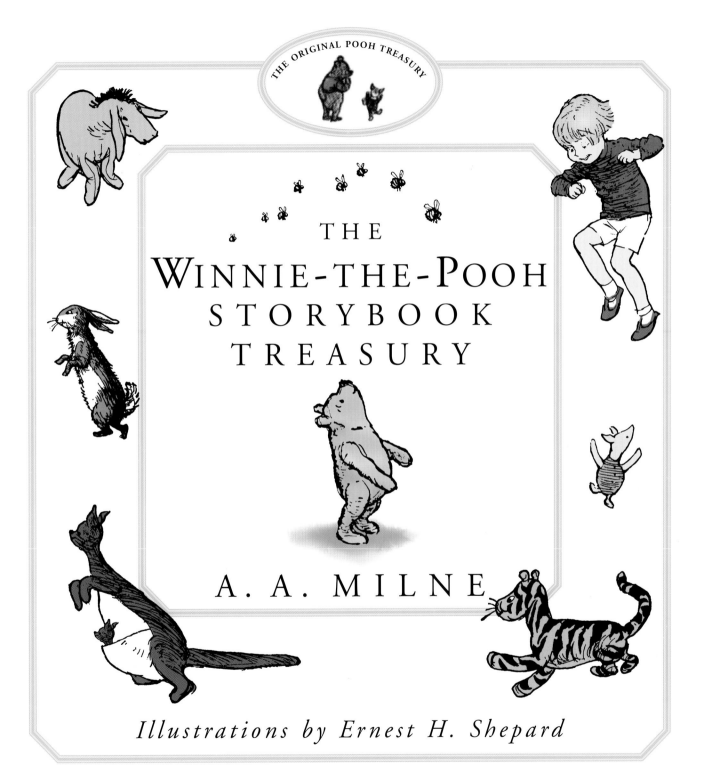

THE ORIGINAL POOH TREASURY

THE
WINNIE-THE-POOH
STORYBOOK
TREASURY

A. A. MILNE

Illustrations by Ernest H. Shepard

Pooh

A. A. MILNE

Piglet Meets
a Heffalump

illustrated by

E. H. SHEPARD

DUTTON CHILDREN'S BOOKS

One day, when Christopher Robin and Winnie-the-Pooh and Piglet were all talking together, Christopher Robin finished the mouthful he was eating and said carelessly: 'I saw a Heffalump to-day, Piglet.'

'What was it doing?' asked Piglet.

'Just lumping along,' said Christopher Robin. 'I don't think it saw *me*.'

'I saw one once,' said Piglet. 'At least, I think I did,' he said. 'Only perhaps it wasn't.'

'So did I,' said Pooh, wondering what a Heffalump was like.

'You don't often see them,'
said Christopher Robin carelessly.

'Not now,' said Piglet.

'Not at this time of year,' said Pooh.

Then they all talked about something else,
until it was time for Pooh and Piglet to go
home together. At first as they stumped along
the path which edged the Hundred Acre Wood,

they didn't say much to each other; but when they came to the stream, and had helped each other across the stepping stones, and were able to walk side by side again over the heather, they

began to talk in a friendly way about this and that, and Piglet said, 'If you see what I mean, Pooh,' and Pooh said, 'It's just what I think myself, Piglet,' and Piglet said, 'But, on the other hand, Pooh, we must remember,' and Pooh said, 'Quite true, Piglet, although I had forgotten it for the moment.' And then, just as they came to the Six Pine Trees, Pooh looked round to see that nobody else was listening, and said in a very solemn voice:

'Piglet, I have decided something.'

'What have you decided, Pooh?'

'I have decided to catch a Heffalump.'

Pooh nodded his head several times as he said this, and waited for Piglet to say 'How?' or 'Pooh, you couldn't!' or something helpful of that sort, but Piglet said nothing. The fact was Piglet was wishing that *he* had thought about it first.

'I shall do it,' said Pooh, after waiting a little longer, 'by means of a trap. And it must be a Cunning Trap, so you will have to help me, Piglet.'

'Pooh,' said Piglet, feeling quite happy again now, 'I will.' And then he said, 'How shall we do it?' and Pooh said, 'That's just it. How?' And then they sat down together to think it out.

Pooh's first idea was that they should dig a Very Deep Pit, and then the Heffalump would come along and fall into the Pit, and—

'Why?' said Piglet.

'Why what?' said Pooh.

'Why would he fall in?'

Pooh rubbed his nose with his paw, and said that the Heffalump might be walking along, humming a little song, and looking up at the sky, wondering if it would rain, and so he wouldn't see the Very Deep Pit until he was half-way down, when it would be too late.

Piglet said that this was a very good Trap, but supposing it were raining already?

Pooh rubbed his nose again, and said that he hadn't thought of that. And then he brightened up, and said that, if it were raining already, the Heffalump would be looking at the sky wondering if it would *clear up*, and so he wouldn't see the Very Deep Pit until he was half-way down. . . . When it would be too late.

Piglet said that, now that this point had been explained, he **thought** it was a Cunning Trap.

Pooh was very proud when he heard this, and he felt that the Heffalump was as good as caught already, but there was just one other thing which had to be thought about, and it was this. *Where should they dig the Very Deep Pit?*

Piglet said that the best place would be somewhere where a Heffalump was, just before he fell into it, only about a foot further on.

'But then he would see us digging it,' said Pooh.

'Not if he was looking at the sky.'

'He would Suspect,' said Pooh, 'if he happened to look down.' He thought for a long time and then added sadly, 'It isn't as easy as I thought. I suppose that's why Heffalumps hardly *ever* get caught.'

'That must be it,' said Piglet.

They sighed and got up; and when they had taken a few gorse prickles out of themselves they sat down again; and all the time Pooh was saying to himself, 'If only I could *think* of something!' For he felt sure that a Very Clever Brain could catch a Heffalump if only he knew the right way to go about it.

'Suppose,' he said to Piglet, '*you* wanted to catch *me*, how would you do it?'

'Well,' said Piglet, 'I should do it like this. I should make a Trap, and I should put a Jar of Honey in the Trap, and you would smell it, and you would go in after it, and—'

'And I would go in after it,' said Pooh excitedly, 'only very carefully so as not to hurt myself, and I would get to the Jar of Honey, and

I should lick round the edges first of all, pretending that there wasn't any more, you know, and then I should walk away and think about it a little, and then I should come back and start licking in the middle of the jar, and then—'

'Yes, well never mind about that. There you would be, and there I should catch you. Now the first thing to think of is, What do Heffalumps like? I should think acorns, shouldn't you? We'll get a lot of—I say, wake up, Pooh!'

Pooh, who had gone into a happy dream, woke up with a start, and said that Honey was a much more trappy thing than Haycorns. Piglet didn't think so; and they were just going to argue about it, when Piglet remembered that, if they put acorns in the Trap, *he* would have to find the acorns, but if they put honey, then Pooh would have to give up some of his own honey, so he said, 'All right, honey then,' just as Pooh remembered it too, and was going to say, 'All right, haycorns.'

'Honey,' said Piglet to himself in a thoughtful way, as if it were now settled. '*I'll* dig the pit, while *you* go and get the honey.'

'Very well,' said Pooh, and he stumped off.

As soon as he got home, he went to the larder; and he stood on a chair, and took down a very large jar of honey from the top shelf. It had HUNNY written on it, but, just to make sure, he took off the paper cover and looked at it, and it *looked* just like honey. 'But you never can tell,' said Pooh. 'I remember my uncle saying once that he had seen cheese just this colour.' So he put his tongue in,

and took a large lick. 'Yes,' he said, 'it is.
No doubt about that. And honey, I should say,
right down to the bottom of the jar. Unless, of
course,' he said, 'somebody put cheese in at the
bottom just for a joke. Perhaps I had better go
a *little* further . . . just in case . . . in case
Heffalumps *don't* like cheese . . . same as me. . . .

Ah!' And he gave a deep sigh. 'I *was* right. It *is* honey, right the way down.'

Having made certain of this, he took the jar back to Piglet, and Piglet looked up from the bottom of his Very Deep Pit, and said, 'Got it?' and Pooh said, 'Yes, but it isn't quite a full jar,' and he threw it down to Piglet, and Piglet said, 'No, it isn't! Is that all you've got left?' and Pooh said, 'Yes.' Because it was. So Piglet put the jar at the bottom of the Pit, and climbed out, and they went off home together.

'Well, good night, Pooh,' said Piglet, when they had got to Pooh's house. 'And we meet at six o'clock tomorrow morning by the Pine Trees, and see how many Heffalumps we've got in our Trap.'

'Six o'clock, Piglet. And have you got any string?'

'No. Why do you want string?'

'To lead them home with.'

'Oh! . . . I *think* Heffalumps come if you whistle.'

'Some do and some don't. You never can tell with Heffalumps. Well, good night!'

'Good night!'

And off Piglet trotted to his house T R E S-P A S S E R S W, while Pooh made his preparations for bed.

Some hours later, just as the night was beginning to steal away,
Pooh woke suddenly
with a sinking feeling. He had had that sinking feeling before, and he knew what it meant.

He was hungry.

So he went to the larder,

and he stood on a chair and reached up to the top shelf, and found – nothing.

'That's funny,' he thought. 'I know I had a jar of honey there. A full jar, full of honey right up to the top, and it had HUNNY written on it, so that I should know it was honey. That's very funny.' And then he began to wander up and down, wondering where it was and murmuring a murmur to himself. Like this:

> It's very, very funny,
> 'Cos I *know* I had some honey;
> 'Cos it had a label on,
>   Saying HUNNY.
>
> A goloptious full-up pot too,
> And I don't know where it's got to,
> No, I don't know where it's gone –
>   Well, it's funny.

He had murmured this to himself three times in a singing sort of way, when suddenly he remembered. He had put it into the Cunning Trap to catch the Heffalump.

'Bother!' said Pooh. 'It all comes of trying

to be kind to Heffalumps.' And he got back
into bed.

But he couldn't sleep. The more he tried to
sleep, the more he couldn't. He tried Counting
Sheep, which is sometimes a good way of
getting to sleep, and, as that was no good, he
tried counting Heffalumps. And that was worse.
Because every Heffalump that he counted
was making straight for a pot of Pooh's honey,

and eating it all. For some minutes he lay there miserably, but when the five hundred and eighty-seventh Heffalump was licking its jaws, and saying to itself, 'Very good honey this, I don't know when I've tasted better,' Pooh could bear it no longer. He jumped out of bed, he ran out of the house, and he ran straight to the Six Pine Trees.

The Sun was still in bed, but there was a lightness in the sky over the Hundred Acre Wood which seemed to show that it was waking up and would soon be kicking off the clothes. In the half-light the Pine Trees looked cold and lonely, and the Very Deep Pit seemed deeper than it was, and Pooh's jar of honey at the bottom was something mysterious, a shape and no more. But as he got nearer to it his nose told him that it was indeed honey, and his tongue came out and began to polish up his mouth, ready for it.

25

'Bother!' said Pooh, as he got his nose inside the jar. 'A Heffalump has been eating it!' And then he thought a little and said, 'Oh, no, *I* did. I forgot.'

Indeed, he had eaten most of it. But there was a little left at the very bottom of the jar, and he pushed

his head

right in,

and began to lick. . . .

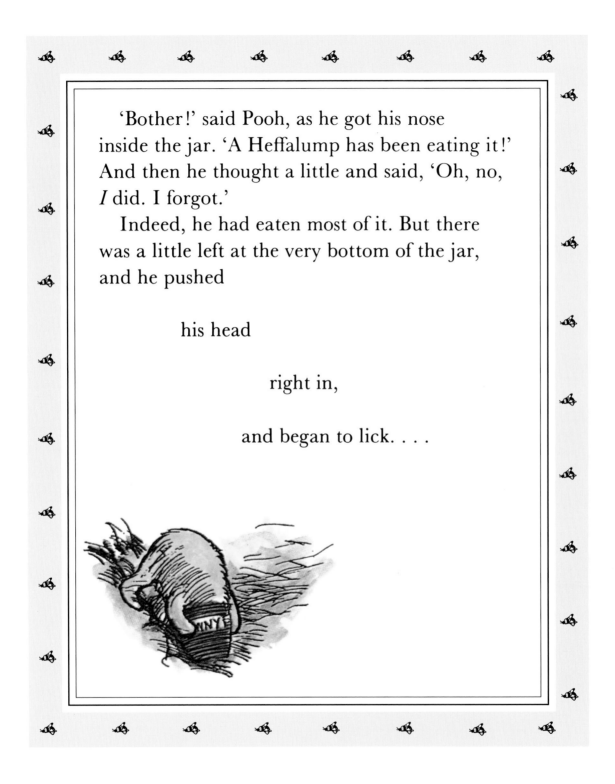

By and by Piglet woke up. As soon as he woke he said to himself, 'Oh!' Then he said bravely, 'Yes,' and then, still more bravely,

'Quite so.' But he didn't feel very brave, for the word which was really jiggeting about in his brain was

'Heffalumps.'

What was a Heffalump like?
Was it Fierce?
Did it come when you whistled? And *how* did it come?
Was it Fond of Pigs at all?

If it was Fond of Pigs, did it make any
difference *what sort of Pig?*
    Supposing
it was Fierce with Pigs,
would it make any difference
if the Pig had a grandfather
called
TRESPASSERS WILLIAM?
    He didn't know the answer
to any of these questions . . .
and he was going to see his first Heffalump
in about an hour from now!
    Of course Pooh would be with him,
and it was much more Friendly with two.
But suppose Heffalumps were Very Fierce
with Pigs *and* Bears?
Wouldn't it be better to pretend
that he had a headache,
and couldn't go
up to the Six Pine Trees this morning?
But then
supposing that it was a very fine day and there

was no Heffalump in the trap, here he would be, in bed all the morning, simply wasting his time for nothing. What should he do?

And then he had a Clever Idea. He would
go up very quietly to the Six Pine Trees now,
peep very cautiously into the Trap,
and see if there *was* a Heffalump there.
And if there was,
he would go back to bed,
and if there wasn't,
he wouldn't.

So off he went. At first he thought that
there wouldn't be a Heffalump in the Trap,
and then he thought that there would, and
as he got nearer he was *sure* that there would,
because he could hear it heffalumping about it
like anything.

'Oh, dear, oh, dear, oh, dear!' said Piglet to
himself. And he wanted to run away.
But somehow, having got so near,
he felt that he must
just see what a Heffalump was like.
So
he crept
to the side of the Trap and looked in. . . .

And all the time Winnie-the-Pooh had been
trying to get the honey-jar off his head.
The more he shook it, the more tightly
it stuck.

'*Bother!*' he said, inside the jar, and '*Oh,
help!*' and, mostly, '*Ow!*' And he tried bumping it against things, but as he couldn't see
what he was bumping it against, it didn't help
him; and he tried to climb out of the Trap, but
as he could see nothing but jar, and not much
of that, he couldn't find his way. So at last he
lifted up his head, jar and all, and made a loud,

roaring noise of Sadness and Despair . . . and
it was at that moment that Piglet looked
down.

   'Help, help!' cried Piglet, 'a Heffalump,
a Horrible Heffalump!' and he scampered off
as hard as he could, still crying out,

      'Help,

          help,

a Herrible Hoffalump! Hoff, Hoff, a Hellible

Horralump! Holl, Holl, a Hoffable Hellerump!'
And he didn't stop crying and scampering
until he got to Christopher Robin's house.

'Whatever's the matter, Piglet?'
said Christopher Robin,
who was just getting up.

'Heff,' said Piglet, breathing so hard
that he could hardly speak, 'a Heff – a Heff –
a Heffalump.'

'Where?'

'Up there,' said Piglet, waving his paw.

'What did it look like?'

'Like – like— It had the biggest head
you ever saw, Christopher Robin. A great
enormous thing, like – like nothing. A huge
big – well, like a – I don't know – like
an enormous big nothing. Like a jar.'

'Well,' said Christopher Robin, putting on
his shoes, 'I shall go and look at it.
Come on.'

Piglet wasn't afraid if he had Christopher
Robin with him, so off they went. . . .

'I can hear it, can't you?' said Piglet anxiously, as they got near.

'I can hear *something*,' said Christopher Robin.

It was Pooh bumping his head against a tree-root he had found.

'There!' said Piglet. 'Isn't it *awful*?' And he held on tight to Christopher Robin's hand.

Suddenly Christopher Robin began to laugh . . .

and he laughed . . .

and he laughed . . .

and he laughed.

And while he was still laughing –

Crash went the Heffalump's head against the tree-root, Smash went the jar, and out came Pooh's head again. . . .

Then Piglet saw what a Foolish Piglet he had been, and he was so ashamed of himself that he ran straight off home and went to bed with a headache. But Christopher Robin and Pooh went home to breakfast together.

'Oh, Bear!' said Christopher Robin. 'How I do love you!'
'So do I,' said Pooh.

Pooh

A. A. MILNE

A House Is Built at Pooh Corner for Eeyore

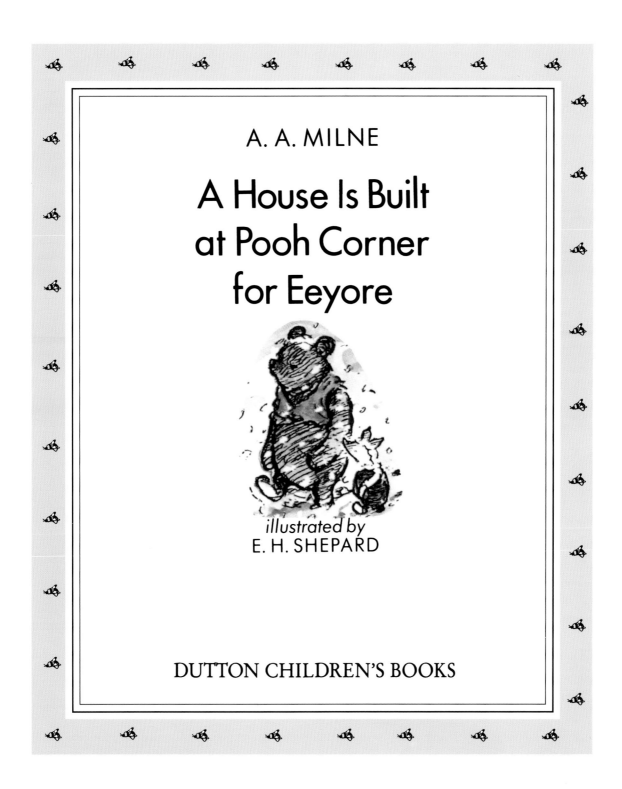

illustrated by
E. H. SHEPARD

DUTTON CHILDREN'S BOOKS

A House Is Built at Pooh Corner for Eeyore

One day when Pooh Bear had nothing else to do, he thought he would do something, so he went round to Piglet's house to see what Piglet was doing. It was still snowing as he stumped over the white forest track, and he expected to find Piglet warming his toes in front of his fire, but to his surprise he saw that the door was open, and the more he looked inside the more Piglet wasn't there.

'He's out,' said Pooh sadly. 'That's what it is. He's not in. I shall have to go a fast Thinking Walk by myself. Bother!'

But first he thought that he would knock very loudly just to make *quite* sure . . . and while he waited for Piglet not to answer, he jumped up and down to keep warm, and a hum came suddenly into his head, which seemed to him a Good Hum, such as is Hummed Hopefully to Others.

The more it snows
    (Tiddely pom),
The more it goes
    (Tiddely pom),
The more it goes
    (Tiddely pom)
On Snowing.
And nobody knows
    (Tiddely pom),
How cold my toes
    (Tiddely pom),
How cold my toes
    (Tiddely pom),
Are growing.

'So what I'll do,' said Pooh, 'is I'll do this. I'll just go home first and see what the time is, and perhaps I'll put a muffler round my neck, and then I'll go and see Eeyore and sing it to him.'

He hurried back to his own house; and his mind was so busy on the way with the hum that he was getting ready for Eeyore that, when he suddenly saw Piglet sitting in his best arm-chair, he could only stand there rubbing his head and wondering whose house he was in.

'Hallo, Piglet,' he said. 'I thought you were out.'

'No,' said Piglet, 'it's you who were out, Pooh.'

'So it was,' said Pooh. 'I knew one of us was.'

He looked up at his clock, which had stopped at five minutes to eleven some weeks ago.

'Nearly eleven o'clock,' said Pooh happily. 'You're just in time for a little smackerel of something,' and he put his head into the cupboard. 'And then we'll go out, Piglet, and sing my song to Eeyore.'

'Which song, Pooh?'

'The one we're going to sing to Eeyore,' explained Pooh.

The clock was still saying five minutes to eleven when Pooh and Piglet set out on their way half an hour later. The wind had dropped, and the snow, tired of rushing round in circles trying to catch itself up, now fluttered gently down until it found a place on which to rest, and sometimes the place was Pooh's nose and sometimes it wasn't and in a little while Piglet was wearing a white muffler round his neck and feeling more snowy behind the ears than he had ever felt before.

'Pooh,' he said at last, and a little timidly, because he didn't want Pooh to think he was Giving In, 'I was just wondering. How would it be if we went home now and *practised* your song, and then sang it to Eeyore to-morrow—or—or the next day, when we happen to see him?'

'That's a very good idea, Piglet,' said Pooh. 'We'll practise it now as we go along. But it's no good going home to practise it, because it's a special Outdoor Song which Has To Be Sung in the Snow.'

'Are you sure?' asked Piglet anxiously.

'Well, you'll see, Piglet, when you listen. Because this is how it begins. *The more it snows, tiddely pom*—'

'Tiddely what?' said Piglet.

'Pom,' said Pooh. 'I put that in to make it more hummy. *The more it goes, tiddely pom, the more*—'

'Didn't you say snows?'

'Yes, but that was *before*.'

'Before the tiddely pom?'

'It was a *different* tiddely pom,' said Pooh,

feeling rather muddled now. 'I'll sing it to you properly and then you'll see.'

So he sang it again.

> The more it
> SNOWS-tiddely-pom,
> The more it
> GOES-tiddely-pom
> The more it
> GOES-tiddely-pom
> On
> Snowing.
>
> And nobody
> KNOWS-tiddely-pom,
> How cold my
> TOES-tiddely-pom
> How cold my
> TOES-tiddely-pom
> Are
> Growing.

He sang it like that, which is much the best way of singing it, and when he had finished, he waited for Piglet to say that, of all the Outdoor Hums for Snowy Weather he had ever heard, this was the best. And, after thinking the matter out carefully, Piglet said:

'Pooh,' he said solemnly, 'it isn't the *toes* so much as the *ears*.'

By this time they were getting near Eeyore's Gloomy Place, which was where he lived, and as it was still very snowy behind Piglet's ears, and he was getting tired of it, they turned into a little pine-wood, and sat down on the gate which led into it. They were out of the snow

now, but it was very cold, and to keep themselves warm they sang Pooh's song right through
six times, Piglet doing the tiddely-poms and
Pooh doing the rest of it, and both of them
thumping on the top of the gate with pieces of
stick at the proper places. And in a little
while they felt much warmer, and were able to
talk again.

'I've been thinking,' said Pooh, 'and what
I've been thinking is this, I've been thinking
about Eeyore.'

'What about Eeyore?'

'Well, poor Eeyore has nowhere to live.'

'Nor he has,' said Piglet.

'*You* have a house, Piglet, and I have a house,

and they are very good houses. And Christopher
Robin has a house, and Owl, and Kanga and

Rabbit have houses, and even Rabbit's friends
and relations have houses or somethings, but
poor Eeyore has nothing. So what I've been
thinking is: Let's build him a house.'

'That,' said Piglet, 'is a Grand Idea. Where
shall we build it?'

'We will build it here,' said Pooh, 'just by
this wood, out of the wind, because this is
where I thought of it. And we will call this
Pooh Corner. And we will build an Eeyore
House with sticks at Pooh Corner for Eeyore.'

'There was a heap of sticks on the other side of the wood,' said Piglet. 'I saw them. Lots and lots. All piled up.'

'Thank you, Piglet,' said Pooh. 'What you have just said will be a Great Help to us, and

because of it I could call the place Poohan-piglet Corner if Pooh Corner didn't sound better, which it does, being smaller and more like a corner. Come along.'

So they got down off the gate and went round to the other side of the wood to fetch the sticks.

Christopher Robin had spent the morning indoors going to Africa and back, and he had just got off the boat and was wondering what it was like outside, when who should come knocking at the door but Eeyore.

'Hallo, Eeyore,' said Christopher Robin, as he opened the door and came out. 'How are *you*?'

'It's snowing still,' said Eeyore gloomily.

'So it is.'

'*And* freezing.'

'Is it?'

'Yes,' said Eeyore. 'However,' he said, brightening up a little, 'we haven't had an earthquake lately.'

'What's the matter, Eeyore?'

'Nothing, Christopher Robin. Nothing important. I suppose you haven't seen a house or what-not anywhere about?'

'What sort of a house?'

'Just a house.'

'Who lives there?'

'I do. At least I thought I did. But I suppose I don't. After all, we can't all have houses.'

'But, Eeyore, I didn't know—I always thought—'

'I don't know how it is, Christopher Robin, but what with all this snow and one thing and another, not to mention icicles and such-like,

it isn't so Hot in my field about three o'clock
in the morning as some people think it is. It
isn't Close, if you know what I mean—not so
as to be uncomfortable. It isn't Stuffy. In
fact, Christopher Robin,' he went on in a loud
whisper, 'quite-between-ourselves-and-don't-
tell-anybody, it's Cold.'

'Oh, Eeyore!'

'And I said to myself: The others will be
sorry if I'm getting myself all cold. They
haven't got Brains, any of them, only grey
fluff that's blown into their heads by mistake,
and they don't Think, but if it goes on snowing

for another six weeks or so, one of them will begin to say to himself, "Eeyore can't be so very much too Hot about three o'clock in the morning." And then it will Get About. And they'll be Sorry.'

'Oh, Eeyore!' said Christopher Robin, feeling very sorry already.

'I don't mean you, Christopher Robin. You're different. So what it all comes to is that I built myself a house down by my little wood.'

'Did you really? How exciting!'

'The really exciting part,' said Eeyore in his most melancholy voice, 'is that when I left

it this morning it was there, and when I came back it wasn't. Not at all, very natural, and it was only Eeyore's house. But still I just wondered.'

Christopher Robin didn't stop to wonder. He was already back in *his* house, putting on his waterproof hat, his waterproof boots, and his waterproof macintosh as fast as he could.

'We'll go and look for it at once,' he called out to Eeyore.

'Sometimes,' said Eeyore, 'when people have quite finished taking a person's house, there are one or two bits which they don't want and are rather glad for the person to take back, if you know what I mean. So I thought if we just went—'

'Come on,' said Christopher Robin, and off they hurried, and in a very little time they got to the corner of the field by the side of the pine-wood, where Eeyore's house wasn't any longer.

'There!' said Eeyore. 'Not a stick of it

left! Of course, I've still got all this snow to do what I like with. One mustn't complain.'

But Christopher Robin wasn't listening to Eeyore, he was listening to something else.

'Can you hear it?' he asked.

'What is it? Somebody laughing?'

'Listen.'

They both listened . . . and they heard a deep gruff voice saying in a singing voice that the more it snowed the more it went on snowing, and a small high voice tiddely-pomming in between.

'It's Pooh,' said Christopher Robin excitedly . . .

'Possibly,' said Eeyore.

'*And* Piglet!' said Christopher Robin excitedly.

'Probably,' said Eeyore. 'What we *want* is a Trained Bloodhound.'

The words of the song changed suddenly.

'*We've finished our* HOUSE!' sang the gruff voice.

'*Tiddely pom!*' sang the squeaky one.

'*It's a beautiful* HOUSE . . .'
'*Tiddely pom* . . .'
'*I wish it were* MINE . . .'
'*Tiddely pom* . . .'
'Pooh!' shouted Christopher Robin . . .

The singers on the gate stopped suddenly.

'It's Christopher Robin!' said Pooh eagerly.

'He's round by the place where we got all those sticks from,' said Piglet.

'Come on,' said Pooh.

They climbed down their gate and hurried round the corner of the wood, Pooh making welcoming noises all the way.

'Why, here *is* Eeyore,' said Pooh, when he had finished hugging Christopher Robin, and he nudged Piglet, and Piglet nudged him, and they thought to themselves what a lovely surprise they had got ready. 'Hallo, Eeyore.'

'Same to you, Pooh Bear, and twice on Thursdays,' said Eeyore gloomily.

Before Pooh could say: 'Why Thursdays?' Christopher Robin began to explain the sad story of Eeyore's Lost House. And Pooh and Piglet listened, and their eyes seemed to get bigger and bigger.

'*Where* did you say it was?' asked Pooh.

'Just here,' said Eeyore.

'Made of sticks?'

'Yes.'

'Oh!' said Piglet.

'What?' said Eeyore.

'I just said "Oh!"' said Piglet nervously. And so as to seem quite at ease he hummed tiddely pom once or twice in a what-shall-we-do-now kind of way.

'You're sure it *was* a house?' said Pooh.

'I mean, you're sure the house was just here?'

'Of course I am,' said Eeyore. And he murmured

to himself, 'No brain at all, some of them.'

'Why, what's the matter, Pooh?' asked Christopher Robin.

'Well,' said Pooh . . . 'The fact *is*,' said Pooh . . . 'Well, the fact *is*,' said Pooh . . . 'You see,' said Pooh . . . 'It's like this,' said Pooh, and something seemed to tell him that he wasn't explaining very well, and he nudged Piglet again.

'It's like this,' said Piglet quickly . . . 'Only warmer,' he added after deep thought.

'What's warmer?'

'The other side of the wood, where Eeyore's house is.'

'*My* house?' said Eeyore. 'My house was here.'

'No,' said Piglet firmly. 'The other side of the wood.'

'Because of being warmer,' said Pooh.

'But I ought to *know*—'

'Come and look,' said Piglet simply, and he led the way.

'There wouldn't be *two* houses,' said Pooh. 'Not so close together.'

They came round the corner, and there was Eeyore's house, looking as comfy as anything.

'There you are,' said Piglet.

'Inside as well as outside,' said Pooh proudly.

Eeyore went inside . . . and came out again.

'It's a remarkable thing,' he said. 'It is my house, and I built it where I said I did, so the wind must have blown it here. And the wind blew it right over the wood, and blew it down here, and here it is as good as ever. In fact, better in places.'

'Much better,' said Pooh and Piglet together.

'It just shows what can be done by taking a

little trouble,' said Eeyore. 'Do you see, Pooh? Do you see, Piglet? Brains first and then Hard

Work. Look at it! *That's* the way to build a house,' said Eeyore proudly.

So they left him in it; and Christopher Robin went back to lunch with his friends Pooh and Piglet, and on the way they told him of the Awful Mistake they had made. And when he had finished laughing, they all sang the Outdoor Song for Snowy Weather the rest of the way home, Piglet, who was still not quite sure of his voice, putting in the tiddely-poms again.

'And I know it *seems* easy,' said Piglet to himself, 'but it isn't *every one* who could do it.'

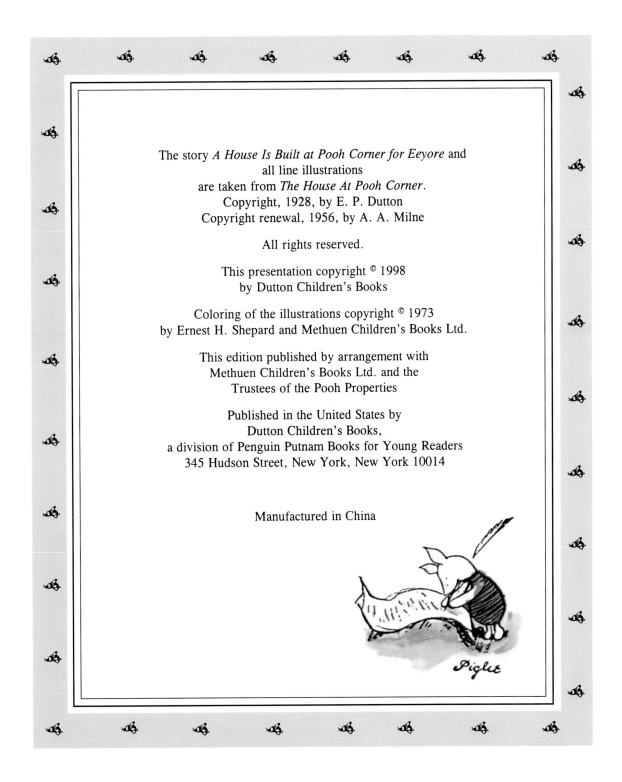

Pooh

A. A. MILNE

Tiggers
Don't
Climb Trees

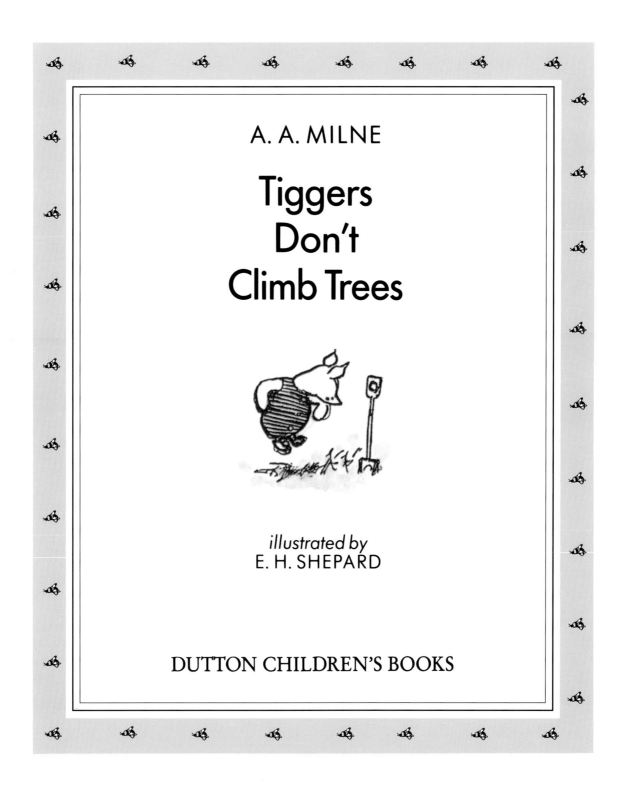

illustrated by
E. H. SHEPARD

DUTTON CHILDREN'S BOOKS

Tiggers Don't Climb Trees

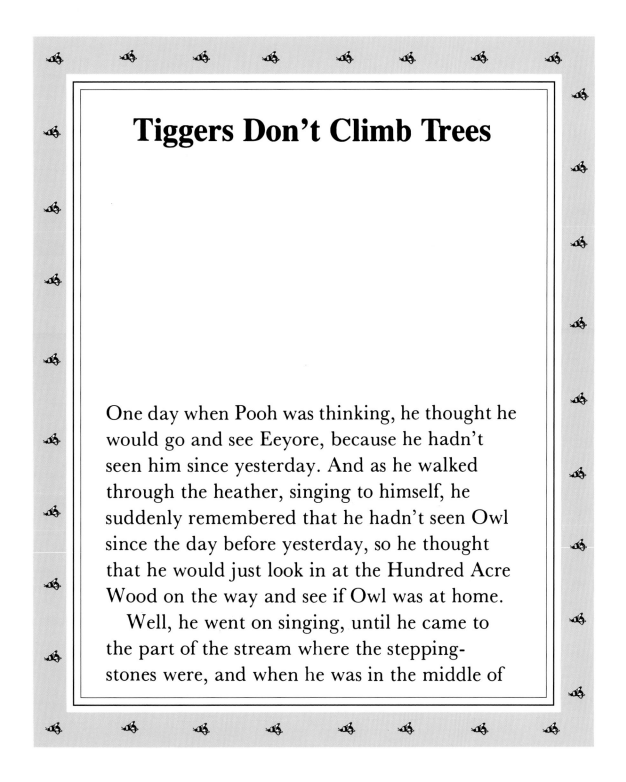

One day when Pooh was thinking, he thought he would go and see Eeyore, because he hadn't seen him since yesterday. And as he walked through the heather, singing to himself, he suddenly remembered that he hadn't seen Owl since the day before yesterday, so he thought that he would just look in at the Hundred Acre Wood on the way and see if Owl was at home.

Well, he went on singing, until he came to the part of the stream where the stepping-stones were, and when he was in the middle of

the third stone he began to wonder how Kanga
and Roo and Tigger were getting on, because
they all lived together in a different part of

the Forest. And he thought, 'I haven't seen Roo for a long time, and if I don't see him to-day it will be a still longer time.' So he sat down on the stone in the middle of the stream, and sang another verse of his song, while he wondered what to do.

The other verse of the song was like this:

> I could spend a happy morning
>   Seeing Roo,
> I could spend a happy morning
>   Being Pooh.
> For it doesn't seem to matter,
> If I don't get any fatter
> (And I *don't* get any fatter),
>   What I do.

The sun was so delightfully warm, and the stone, which had been sitting in it for a long time, was so warm, too, that Pooh had almost decided to go on being Pooh in the middle of

the stream for the rest of the morning, when
he remembered Rabbit.

'Rabbit,' said Pooh to himself. 'I *like*
talking to Rabbit. He talks about sensible things.
He doesn't use long, difficult words, like Owl.
He uses short, easy words, like "What about
lunch?" and "Help yourself, Pooh," I suppose,
really, I ought to go and see Rabbit.'

Which made him think of another verse:

> Oh, I like his way of talking,
>   Yes, I do.
> It's the nicest way of talking
>   Just for two.
> And a Help-yourself with Rabbit
> Though it may become a habit,
> Is a *pleasant* sort of habit
>   For a Pooh.

So when he had sung this, he got up off
his stone, walked back across the stream, and
set off for Rabbit's house.

But he hadn't got far before he began to
say to himself: 'Yes, but suppose Rabbit is out?'

'Or suppose I get stuck in his front door
again, coming out, as I did once when his front
door wasn't big enough?'

'Because I *know* I'm not getting fatter, but
his front door may be getting thinner.'

'So wouldn't it be better if—'

And all the time he was saying things like
this he was going more and more westerly,
without thinking . . . until suddenly he found
himself at his own front
door again.

And it was eleven o'clock.

Which was Time-for-a-
little-something. . . .

Half an hour later he
was doing what he had
always really meant to
do, he was stumping
off to Piglet's house.
And as he walked, he

wiped his mouth with the back of his paw, and
sang rather a fluffy song through the fur. It
went like this:

> I could spend a happy morning
>   Seeing Piglet.
> And I couldn't spend a happy morning
>   Not seeing Piglet.
> And it doesn't seem to matter
> If I don't see Owl and Eeyore (or any of the others),
> And I'm not going to see Owl or Eeyore (or any of
>   the others)
> Or Christopher Robin.

Written down like this, it doesn't seem
a very good song, but coming through pale fawn
fluff at about half-past eleven on a very
sunny morning, it seemed to Pooh to be one of
the best songs he had ever sung. So he went on
singing it.

Piglet was busy digging a small hole in
the ground outside his house.

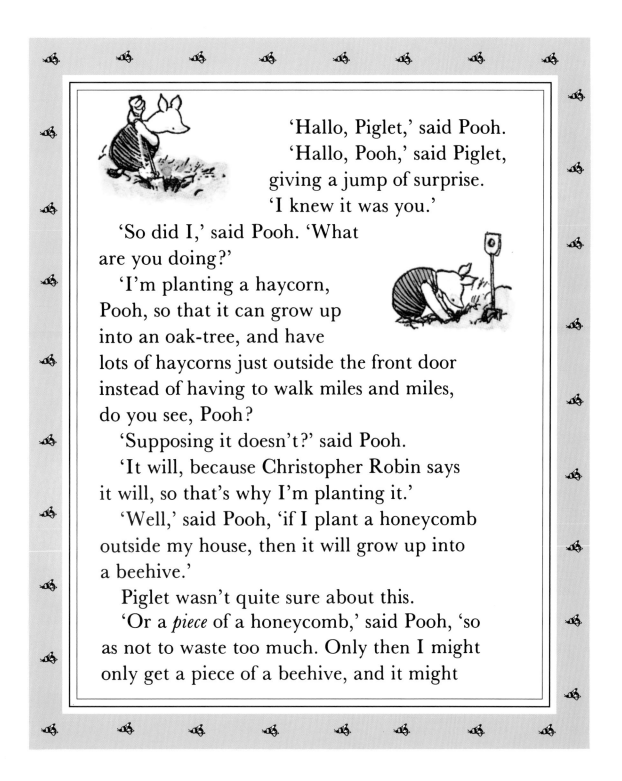

'Hallo, Piglet,' said Pooh.

'Hallo, Pooh,' said Piglet, giving a jump of surprise. 'I knew it was you.'

'So did I,' said Pooh. 'What are you doing?'

'I'm planting a haycorn, Pooh, so that it can grow up into an oak-tree, and have lots of haycorns just outside the front door instead of having to walk miles and miles, do you see, Pooh?

'Supposing it doesn't?' said Pooh.

'It will, because Christopher Robin says it will, so that's why I'm planting it.'

'Well,' said Pooh, 'if I plant a honeycomb outside my house, then it will grow up into a beehive.'

Piglet wasn't quite sure about this.

'Or a *piece* of a honeycomb,' said Pooh, 'so as not to waste too much. Only then I might only get a piece of a beehive, and it might be the wrong piece, where the bees were buzzing and not hunnying. Bother.'

Piglet agreed that that would be rather bothering.

'Besides, Pooh, it's a very difficult thing, planting unless you know how to do it,' he said; and he put the acorn in the hole he had made, and covered it up with earth, and jumped on it.

'I do know,' said Pooh, 'because Christopher Robin gave me a mastershalum seed, and I planted it, and I'm going to have mastershalums all over the front door.'

'I thought they were called nasturtiums,' said Piglet timidly, as he went on jumping.

'No,' said Pooh. 'Not these. These are called mastershalums.'

When Piglet had finished jumping, he wiped his paws on his front, and said, 'What shall we do now?' and Pooh said, 'Let's go and see Kanga and Roo and Tigger,' and Piglet said 'Y-yes. L-let's'—because he was still a little anxious about Tigger, who was a very Bouncy Animal, with a way of saying How-do-you-do, which always left your ears full of sand, even after Kanga had said, 'Gently, Tigger dear,' and had helped you up again. So they set off for Kanga's house.

Now it happened that Kanga had felt rather motherly that morning, and Wanting to Count Things—like Roo's vests, and how many pieces of soap there were left, and the two clean

spots in Tigger's feeder; so she had sent them out with a packet of watercress sandwiches for Roo and a packet of extract-of-malt sandwiches for Tigger, to have a nice long morning in the Forest not getting into mischief. And off they had gone.

And as they went, Tigger told Roo (who wanted to know) all about the things that Tiggers could do.

'Can they fly?' asked Roo.

'Yes,' said Tigger, 'they're very good flyers, Tiggers are. Strornry good flyers.'

'Oo!' said Roo. 'Can they fly as well as Owl?'

'Yes,' said Tigger. 'Only they don't want to.'

'Why don't they want to?'

'Well, they just don't like it, somehow.'

Roo couldn't understand this, because he thought it would be lovely to be able to fly, but Tigger said it was difficult to explain to anybody who wasn't a Tigger himself.

'Well,' said Roo, 'can they jump as far as Kangas?'

'Yes,' said Tigger. 'When they want to.'

'I *love* jumping,' said Roo. 'Let see who can jump farthest, you or me.'

'*I* can,' said Tigger. 'But we mustn't stop now, or we shall be late.'

'Late for what?'

'For whatever we want to be in time for,' said Tigger, hurrying on.

In a little while they came to the Six Pine Trees.

'I can swim,' said Roo. 'I fell into the river, and I swimmed. Can Tiggers swim?'

'Of course they can. Tiggers can do everything.'

'Can they climb trees better than Pooh?' asked Roo, stopping under the tallest Pine Tree, and looking up at it.

'Climbing trees is what they do best,' said Tigger. 'Much better than Poohs.'

'Could they climb this one?'

'They're always climbing trees like that,' said Tigger. 'Up and down all day.'

'Oo, Tigger, are they *really*?'

'I'll show you,' said Tigger bravely, 'and you can sit on my back and watch me.' For of all the things which he had said Tiggers could do, the only one he felt really certain about suddenly was climbing trees.

'Oo, Tigger—oo, Tigger—oo, Tigger!' squeaked Roo excitedly.

So he sat on Tigger's back and up they went.

And for the first ten feet Tigger said happily to himself, 'Up we go!'

And for the next ten feet he said: 'I always *said* Tiggers could climb trees.'

And for the next ten feet he said: 'Not that it's easy, mind you.'

And for the next ten feet he said: 'Of course, there's the coming-down too. Backwards.'

And then he said: 'Which will be difficult . . .'

'Unless one fell . . .'

'When it would be . . .'

'EASY.'

And at the word 'easy', the branch he was standing on broke suddenly and he just managed to clutch at the one above him as he felt himself going . . . and then slowly he got his chin over it . . . and then one back paw . . . and then the other . . . until at last he was sitting on it, breathing very quickly, and wishing that he had gone in for swimming instead.

Roo climbed off, and sat down next to him.

'Oo, Tigger,' he said excitedly, 'are we at the top?'

'No,' said Tigger.

'Are we going to the top?'

'*No*,' said Tigger.

'Oh!' said Roo rather sadly. And then he went on hopefully: 'That was a lovely bit just now, when you pretended we were going to fall-bump-to-the-bottom, and we didn't. Will you do that bit again?'

'NO,' said Tigger.

Roo was silent for a little while, and then he said, 'Shall we eat our sandwiches, Tigger?' And

Tigger said, 'Yes, where are they?' And Roo said, 'At the bottom of the tree.'

And Tigger said, 'I don't think we'd better eat them just yet.'

So they didn't.

By-and-by Pooh and Piglet came along. Pooh was telling Piglet in a singing voice that it didn't seem to matter, if he didn't get any fatter, and he didn't *think* he was getting any fatter, what he did; and Piglet was wondering how long it would be before his haycorn came up.

'Look, Pooh!' said Piglet suddenly. 'There's something in one of the Pine Trees.'

'So there is!' said Pooh, looking up wonderingly. 'There's an Animal.'

Piglet took Pooh's arm, in case Pooh was frightened. 'Is it One of the Fiercer Animals?' he said, looking the other way.

Pooh nodded. 'It's a Jagular,' he said.

'What do Jagulars do?' asked Piglet, hoping that they wouldn't.

'They hide in the branches of trees and drop on you as you go underneath,' said Pooh. 'Christopher Robin told me.'

'Perhaps we better hadn't go underneath, Pooh. In case he dropped and hurt himself.'

'They don't hurt themselves,' said Pooh. 'They're such very good droppers.'

Piglet still felt that to be underneath a Very Good Dropper would be a Mistake, and he was just going to hurry back for something which he had forgotten when the Jagular called out to them.

'Help! Help!' it called.

'That's what Jagulars always do,' said Pooh, much interested. 'They call "Help! Help!" and then when you look up, they drop on you.'

'I'm looking *down*,' cried Piglet loudly, so as the Jagular shouldn't do the wrong thing by accident.

Something very excited next to the Jagular heard him, and squeaked: 'Pooh and Piglet! Pooh and Piglet!'

All of a sudden Piglet felt that it was a much nicer day than he had thought it was. All warm and sunny—

'Pooh!' he cried. 'I believe it's Tigger and Roo!'

'So it is,' said Pooh. 'I thought it was a Jagular and another Jagular.'

'Hallo, Roo!' called Piglet. 'What are you doing?'

'We can't get down, we can't get down!' cried

Roo. 'Isn't it fun? Pooh, isn't it fun, Tigger and I are living in a tree, like Owl, and we're going to stay here for ever and ever. I can see Piglet's house. Piglet, I can see your house from here. Aren't we high? Is Owl's house as high up as this?'

'How did you get there, Roo?' asked Piglet.

'On Tigger's back! And Tiggers can't climb downwards, because their tails get in the way, only upwards, and Tigger forgot about that when

we started, and he's only just remembered. So
we've got to stay here for ever and ever—
unless we go higher. What did you say, Tigger?
Oh, Tigger says if we go higher we shan't be
able to see Piglet's house so well, so we're
going to stop here.'

'Piglet,' said Pooh solemnly, when he had
heard all this, 'what shall we do?' And he began
to eat Tigger's sandwiches.

'Are they stuck?' asked Piglet anxiously.

Pooh nodded.

'Couldn't you climb up to them?'

'I might, Piglet, and I might bring Roo down

on my back, but I couldn't bring Tigger down. So we must think of something else.' And in a thoughtful way he began to eat Roo's sandwiches, too.

Whether he would have thought of anything before he had finished the last sandwich, I don't know, but he had just got to the last but one when there was a crackling in the bracken, and Christopher Robin and Eeyore came strolling along together.

'I shouldn't be surprised if it hailed a good deal to-morrow,' Eeyore was saying. 'Blizzards and what-not. Being fine to-day doesn't Mean Anything. It has no sig—what's that word? Well, it has none of that. It's just a small piece of weather.'

'There's Pooh!' said Christopher Robin, who didn't much mind *what* it did to-morrow, as long as he was out in it. 'Hallo, Pooh!'

'It's Christopher Robin!'

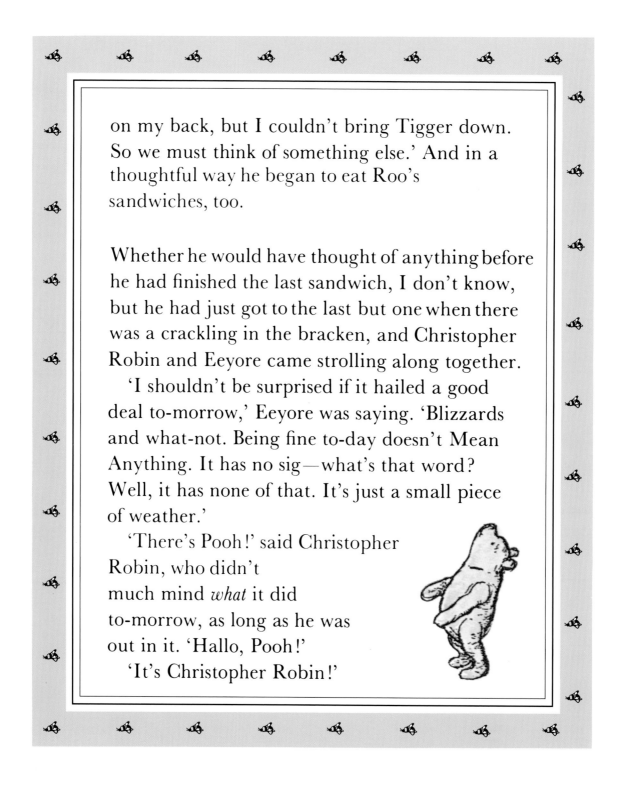

said Piglet. '*He'll* know what to do.'

They hurried up to him.

'Oh, Christopher Robin,' began Pooh.

'And Eeyore,' said Eeyore.

'Tigger and Roo are right up the Six Pine Trees, and they can't get down, and—'

'And I was just saying,' put in Piglet, 'that if only Christopher Robin—'

'*And* Eeyore—'

'If only you were here, then we could think of something to do.'

Christopher Robin looked up at Tigger and Roo, and tried to think of something.

'*I* thought,' said Piglet earnestly, 'that if Eeyore stood at the bottom of the tree, and if Pooh stood on Eeyore's back, and if I stood on Pooh's shoulders—'

'And if Eeyore's back snapped suddenly, then we could all laugh. Ha ha! Amusing in a quiet way,' said Eeyore, 'but not really helpful.'

'Well,' said Piglet meekly, '*I* thought—'

'Would it break your back, Eeyore?' asked

Pooh, very much surprised.

'That's what would be so interesting, Pooh. Not being quite sure till afterwards.'

Pooh said 'Oh!' and they all began to think again.

'I've got an idea!' cried Christopher Robin suddenly.

'Listen to this, Piglet,' said Eeyore, 'and then you'll know what we're trying to do.'

'I'll take off my tunic and we'll each hold a corner, and then Roo and Tigger can jump into it, and it will be all soft and bouncy for them, and they won't hurt themselves.'

'*Getting Tigger down*,' said Eeyore, 'and *Not hurting anybody*. Keep those two ideas in your head, Piglet, and you'll be all right.'

But Piglet wasn't listening, he was so agog at the thought of seeing Christopher Robin's blue braces again. He had only seen them once before, when he was much younger, and, being a little over-excited by them, had had to go to bed half an hour earlier than usual; and he had always wondered since if they were *really* as blue and as bracing as he had thought them. So when Christopher Robin took his tunic off, and they were, he felt quite friendly to Eeyore again, and held the corner of the tunic next to him and smiled happily at him. And Eeyore whispered back: 'I'm not saying there won't be an Accident *now*, mind you. They're funny things, Accidents. You never have them till you're having them.'

When Roo understood what he had to do, he was wildly excited and cried out: 'Tigger, Tigger, we're going to jump! Look at me jumping, Tigger! Like flying, my jumping will be. Can Tiggers do it?' And he squeaked out: 'I'm coming, Christopher Robin!' and he jumped— straight into the middle of the tunic. And he was going so fast that he bounced up again almost as high as where he was before—and he went on

bouncing and saying, 'Oo!' for quite a long time
—and then at last he stopped and said, 'Oo,
lovely!' And they put him on the ground.

'Come on, Tigger,' he called out. 'It's easy.'

But Tigger was holding on to the branch and
saying to himself: 'It's all very well for
Jumping Animals like Kangas, but it's quite
different for Swimming Animals like Tiggers.'
And he thought of himself floating on his back
down a river, or striking out from one island to
another, and he felt that that was really the
life for a Tigger.

'Come along,' called Christopher Robin.
'You'll be all right.'

'Just wait a moment,' said Tigger nervously.
'Small piece of bark in my eye.' And he moved
slowly along his branch.

'Come on, it's easy!' squeaked Roo. And
suddenly Tigger found how easy it was.

'Ow!' he shouted as the tree flew past him.

'Look out!' cried Christopher Robin to the
others.

There was a crash, and a tearing noise, and a confused heap of everybody on the ground.

Christopher Robin and Pooh and Piglet picked themselves up first, and then they picked Tigger up, and underneath everybody else was Eeyore.

'Oh, Eeyore!' cried Christopher Robin. 'Are you hurt?' And he felt him rather anxiously, and dusted him and helped him to stand up again.

Eeyore said nothing for a long time. And then he said: 'Is Tigger there?'

Tigger was there, feeling Bouncy again already.

'Yes,' said Christopher Robin. 'Tigger's here.'

'Well, just thank him for me,' said Eeyore.

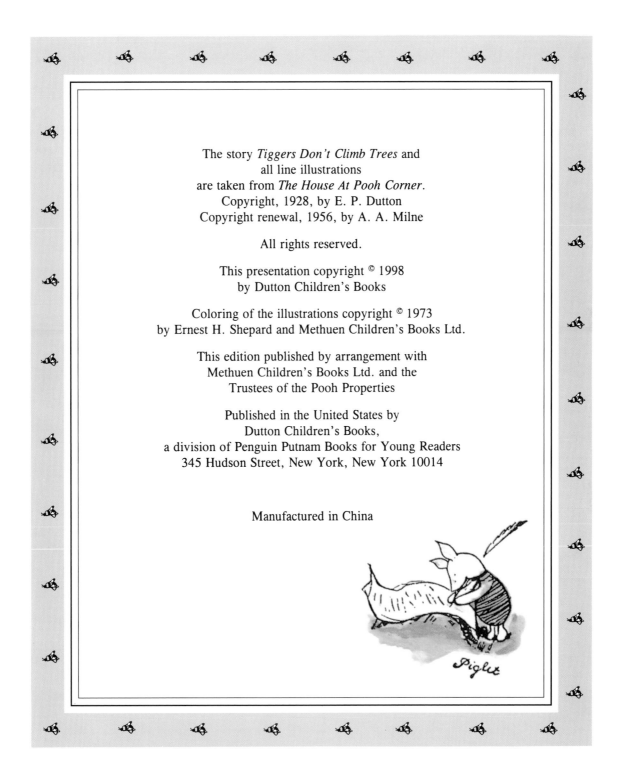

Pooh

98

A. A. MILNE

Winnie-the-Pooh and Some Bees

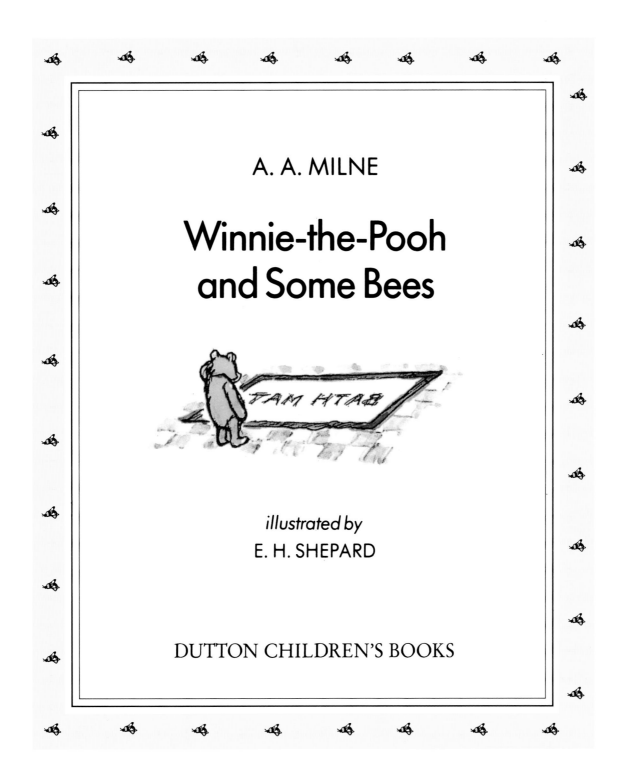

illustrated by

E. H. SHEPARD

DUTTON CHILDREN'S BOOKS

Winnie-the-Pooh
and Some Bees

Here is Edward Bear, coming downstairs now, bump, bump, bump, on the back of his head, behind Christopher Robin. It is, as far as he knows, the only way of coming downstairs, but sometimes he feels that there really is another way, if only he could stop bumping for a moment and think of it. And then he feels that perhaps there isn't. Anyhow, here he is at the bottom, and ready to be introduced to you. Winnie-the-Pooh.

When I first heard his name, I said, just as you are going to say, 'But I thought he was a boy?'

'So did I,' said Christopher Robin.

'Then you can't call him Winnie?'

'I don't.'

'But you said—'

'He's Winnie-ther-Pooh. Don't you know what "*ther*" means?'

'Ah, yes, now I do,' I said quickly; and I hope you do too, because it is all the explanation you are going to get.

Sometimes Winnie-the-Pooh likes a game of some sort when he comes downstairs,

and sometimes he likes to sit quietly in
front of the fire and listen to a story. This
evening—

    'What about a story?' said Christopher Robin.

    '*What* about a story?' I said.

    'Could you very sweetly tell Winnie-the-Pooh
one?'

    'I suppose I could,' I said. 'What sort of
stories does he like?'

    'About himself. Because he's *that* sort of Bear.'

    'Oh, I see.'

    'So could you very sweetly?'

    'I'll try,' I said.

So I tried.

    Once upon a time, a very long time ago now,
about last Friday, Winnie-the-Pooh lived in a
forest all by himself under the name of Sanders.

    *('What does "under the name" mean?' asked
Christopher Robin.*

    *'It means he had the name over the door in gold
letters and lived under it.'*

'Winnie-the-Pooh wasn't quite sure,' said Christopher Robin.

'Now I am,' said a growly voice.

'Then I will go on,' said I.)

One day when he was out walking, he came to an open place in the middle of the forest, and in the middle of this place was a large oak-tree, and, from the top of the tree, there came a loud buzzing-noise.

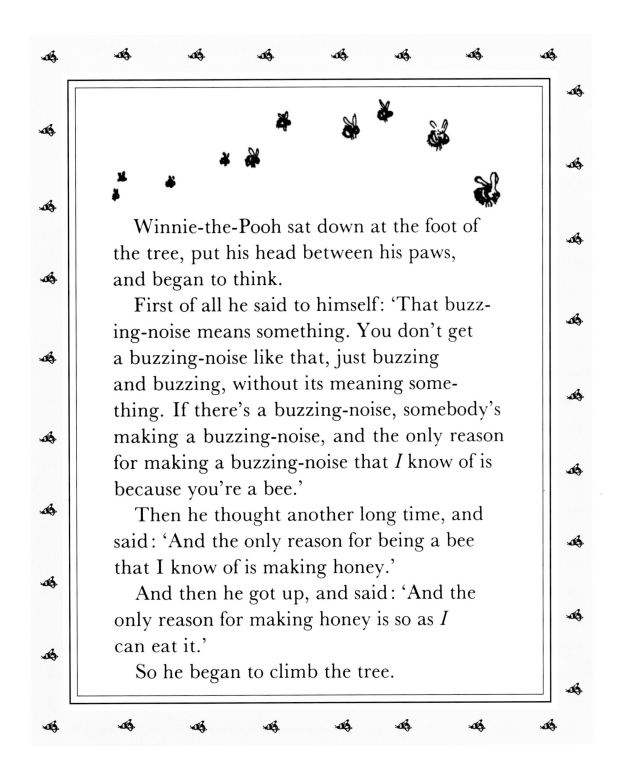

Winnie-the-Pooh sat down at the foot of the tree, put his head between his paws, and began to think.

First of all he said to himself: 'That buzzing-noise means something. You don't get a buzzing-noise like that, just buzzing and buzzing, without its meaning something. If there's a buzzing-noise, somebody's making a buzzing-noise, and the only reason for making a buzzing-noise that *I* know of is because you're a bee.'

Then he thought another long time, and said: 'And the only reason for being a bee that I know of is making honey.'

And then he got up, and said: 'And the only reason for making honey is so as *I* can eat it.'

So he began to climb the tree.

He
climbed
and he
climbed
and he
climbed,
and
as he
climbed
he sang
a little
song
to
himself.
It
went
like
this:

Isn't it funny
How a bear likes honey?
Buzz! Buzz! Buzz!
I wonder why he does?

Then he climbed a little further . . . and a little further . . . and then just a little further. By that time he had thought of another song.

It's a very funny thought that, if Bears were Bees,
They'd build their nests at the *bottom* of trees.
And that being so (if the Bees were Bears),
We shouldn't have to climb up all these stairs.

He was getting rather tired by this time, so that is why he sang a Complaining Song. He was nearly there now, and if he just stood on that branch . . . *Crack!*

'Oh, help!' said Pooh, as he dropped ten feet on the branch below him.

'If only I hadn't—' he said, as he bounced twenty feet on to the next branch.

'You see, what I *meant* to do,' he explained, as he turned head-over-heels, and crashed on to another branch thirty feet below, 'what I *meant* to do—'

'Of course, it *was* rather—' he admitted, as he slithered very quickly through the next six branches.

'It all comes, I suppose,' he decided, as he said good-bye to the last branch, spun round three times, and flew gracefully into a gorse-bush,

'it all comes of *liking* honey so much. Oh, help!'
He crawled out of the gorse-bush, brushed

the prickles from his nose, and began to think
again. And the first person he thought of was
Christopher Robin.

*('Was that me?' said Christopher Robin in an
awed voice, hardly daring to believe it.*

'That was you.'

*Christopher Robin said nothing, but his eyes
got larger and larger, and his face got pinker and
pinker.)*

So Winnie-the-Pooh went round to his friend Christopher Robin, who lived behind a green door in another part of the Forest.

'Good morning, Christopher Robin,' he said.

'Good morning, Winnie-*ther*-Pooh,' said you.

'I wonder if you've got such a thing as a balloon about you?'

'A balloon?'

'Yes, I just said to myself coming along: "I wonder if Christopher Robin has such a thing as a balloon about him?" I just said it to myself, thinking of balloons, and wondering.'

'What do you want a balloon for?' you said.

Winnie-the-Pooh looked round to see that nobody was listening, put his paw to his mouth, and said in a deep whisper: *'Honey!'*

'But you don't get honey with balloons!'

'*I* do,' said Pooh.

Well, it just happened that you had been to a party the day before at the house of your friend Piglet, and you had balloons at the party. You had had a big green balloon; and one of Rabbit's relations had had a big blue one,

and had left it behind, being really too young to go to a party at all; and so you had brought the green one *and* the blue one home with you.

'Which one would you like?' you asked Pooh.

He put his head between his paws and thought very carefully.

'It's like this,' he said. 'When you go after honey with a balloon, the great thing is not to let the bees know you're coming. Now, if you have a green balloon, they might think you were only part of the tree, and not notice you, and if you have a blue balloon, they might think you were only part of the sky, and not notice you, and the question is: Which is most likely?'

'Wouldn't they notice *you* underneath the balloon?' you asked.

'They might or they might not,' said Winnie-the-Pooh. 'You never can tell with bees.' He thought for a moment and said: 'I shall try to look like a small black cloud. That will deceive them.'

'Then you had better have the blue balloon,' you said; and so it was decided.

Well, you both went out with the blue balloon, and you took your gun with you, just in case, as you always did, and Winnie-the-Pooh went to a very muddy place that he knew of, and

rolled and rolled until he was black all over; and

then, when the balloon was blown up as big as big, and you and Pooh were both holding on to the string, you let go suddenly, and Pooh

Bear floated gracefully up into the sky, and stayed there – level with the top of the tree and about twenty feet away from it.

'Hooray!' you shouted.

'Isn't that fine?' shouted Winnie-the-Pooh down to you. 'What do I look like?'

'You look like a Bear holding on to a balloon,' you said.

'Not,' said Pooh anxiously, '—not like a small black cloud in a blue sky?'

'Not very much.'

'Ah, well, perhaps from up here it looks different. And, as I say, you never can tell with bees.'

There was no wind to blow him nearer to the tree so there he stayed. He could see the honey, he could smell the honey, but he couldn't quite reach the honey.

After a little while he called down to you.

'Christopher Robin!' he said in a loud whisper.

'Hallo!'

'I think the bees *suspect* something!'

'What sort of thing?'

'I don't know. But something tells me that they're *suspicious*!'

'Perhaps they think that you're after their honey?'

'It may be that. You never can tell with bees.'

There was another little silence, and then he called down to you again.

'Christopher Robin!'

'Yes?'

'Have you an umbrella in your house?'

'I think so.'

'I wish you would bring it out here, and walk up and down with it, and look up at me every now and then, and say "Tut-tut, it looks like rain." I think, if you did that, it would help the deception which we are practising on these bees.'

Well, you laughed to yourself, 'Silly old Bear!' but you didn't say it aloud because you were so fond of him, and you went home for your umbrella.

'Oh, there you are!' called down Winnie-

the-Pooh, as soon as you got back to the tree.
'I was beginning to get anxious. I have
discovered that the bees are now definitely
Suspicious.'

'Shall I put my umbrella up?' you said.

'Yes, but wait a moment. We must be
practical. The important bee to deceive is the
Queen Bee. Can you see which is the Queen
Bee from down there?'

'No.'

'A pity. Well, now, if you walk up and down
with your umbrella, saying, "Tut-tut, it looks like
rain," I shall do what I can by singing a little
Cloud Song, such as a cloud might sing. . . . Go!'

So, while you walked up and down and wondered if it would rain, Winnie-the-Pooh sang this song:

How sweet to be a Cloud
   Floating in the Blue!
Every little cloud
Always sings aloud.

'How sweet to be a Cloud
   Floating in the Blue!'
It makes him very proud
To be a little cloud.

The bees were still buzzing as suspiciously as ever. Some of them, indeed, left their nests and flew all round the cloud as it began the second verse of this song, and one bee sat down on the nose of the cloud for a moment, and then got up again.

'Christopher – *ow!* – Robin,' called out the cloud.

'Yes?'

'I have just been thinking, and I have come to a very important decision. *These are the wrong sort of bees.*'

'Are they?'

'Quite the wrong sort. So I should think they would make the wrong sort of honey, shouldn't you?'

'Would they?'

'Yes. So I think I shall come down.'

'How?' asked you.

Winnie-the-Pooh hadn't thought about this. If he let go of the string, he would fall – *bump* – and he didn't like the idea of that. So he thought

for a long time, and then he said:

'Christopher Robin, you must shoot the bal-
.loon with your gun. Have you got your gun?'

'Of course I have,' you said. 'But if I do that,
it will spoil the balloon,' you said.

'But if you *don't*,' said Pooh, 'I shall have to
let go, and that would spoil *me*.'

When he put it like this, you saw how it was, and you aimed very carefully at the balloon, and fired.

'*Ow!*' said Pooh.

'Did I miss?' you asked.

'You didn't exactly *miss*,' said Pooh, 'but you missed the *balloon*.'

'I'm so sorry,' you said, and you fired again, and this time you hit the balloon, and the air came slowly out, and Winnie-the-Pooh floated down to the ground.

But his arms were so stiff from holding on to the

string of the balloon all that time that they stayed up straight in the air for more than a week, and whenever a fly came and settled on his nose he had to blow it off. And I think – but I am not sure – that *that* is why he was always called Pooh.

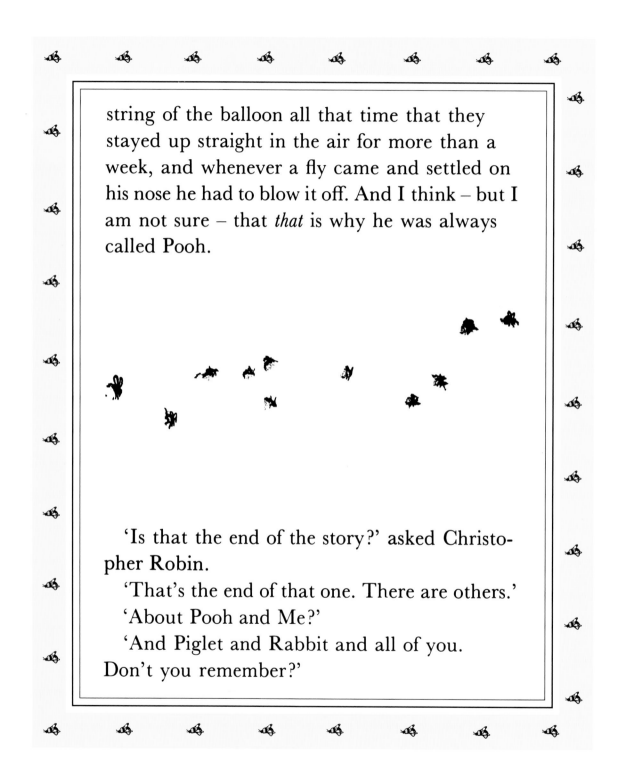

'Is that the end of the story?' asked Christopher Robin.

'That's the end of that one. There are others.'

'About Pooh and Me?'

'And Piglet and Rabbit and all of you. Don't you remember?'

'I do remember, and then when I try to remember, I forget.'

'That day when Pooh and Piglet tried to catch the Heffalump—'

'They didn't catch it, did they?'

'No.'

'Pooh couldn't, because he hasn't any brain. Did *I* catch it?'

'Well, that comes into the story.'

Christopher Robin nodded.

'I do remember,' he said, 'only Pooh doesn't very well, so that's why he likes having it told to him again. Because then it's a real story and not just a remembering.'

'That's just how *I* feel,' I said.

Christopher Robin gave a deep sigh, picked his Bear up by the leg, and walked off to the door, trailing Pooh behind him. At the door he turned and said, 'Coming to see me have my bath?'

'I might,' I said.

'I didn't hurt him when I shot him, did I?'

'Not a bit.'

He nodded and went out, and in a moment I heard Winnie-the-Pooh – *bump, bump, bump* – going up the stairs behind him.

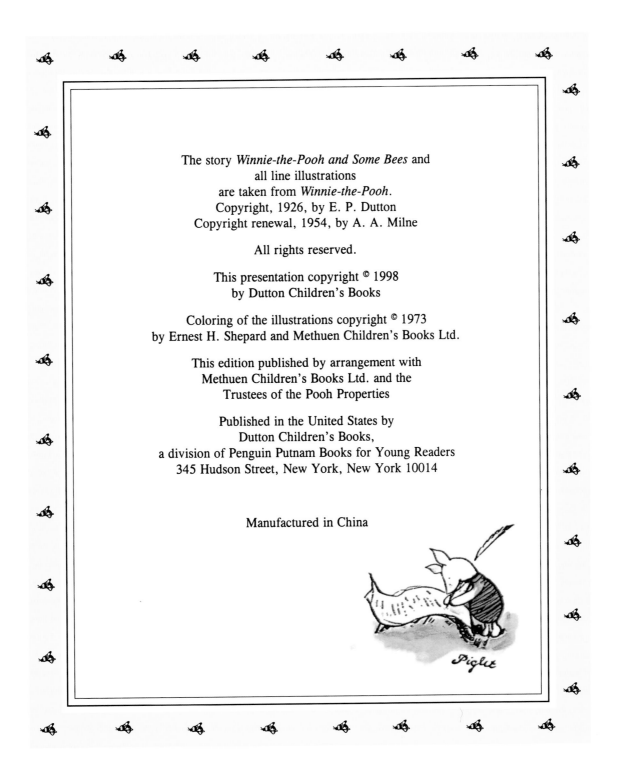

Pooh

A. A. MILNE

Eeyore
Has a Birthday

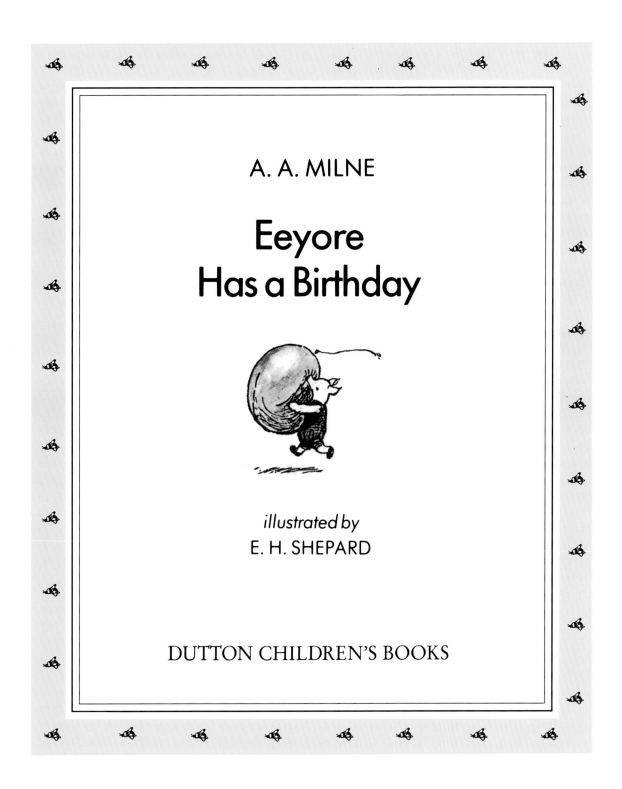

illustrated by
E. H. SHEPARD

DUTTON CHILDREN'S BOOKS

Eeyore Has a Birthday

Eeyore, the old grey Donkey, stood by the side of the stream, and looked at himself in the water.

'Pathetic,' he said. 'That's what it is. Pathetic.'

He turned and walked slowly down the stream for twenty yards, splashed across it, and walked slowly back on the other side. Then he looked at himself in the water again.

'As I thought,' he said. 'No better from *this* side. But nobody minds. Nobody cares. Pathetic, that's what it is.'

There was a crackling noise in the bracken behind him, and out came Pooh.

'Good morning, Eeyore,' said Pooh.

'Good morning, Pooh Bear,' said Eeyore gloomily. 'If it *is* a good morning,' he said. 'Which I doubt,' said he.

'Why, what's the matter?'

'Nothing, Pooh Bear, nothing. We can't all, and some of us don't. That's all there is to it.'

'Can't all *what*?' said Pooh, rubbing his nose.

'Gaiety. Song-and-dance. Here we go round the mulberry bush.'

'Oh!' said Pooh. He thought for a long time, and then asked, 'What mulberry bush is that?'

'Bon-hommy,' went on Eeyore gloomily. 'French word meaning bonhommy,' he explained. 'I'm not complaining, but There It Is.'

Pooh sat down on a large stone, and tried to think this out. It sounded to him like a riddle, and he was never much good at riddles, being a Bear of Very Little Brain. So he sang *Cottleston Pie* instead:

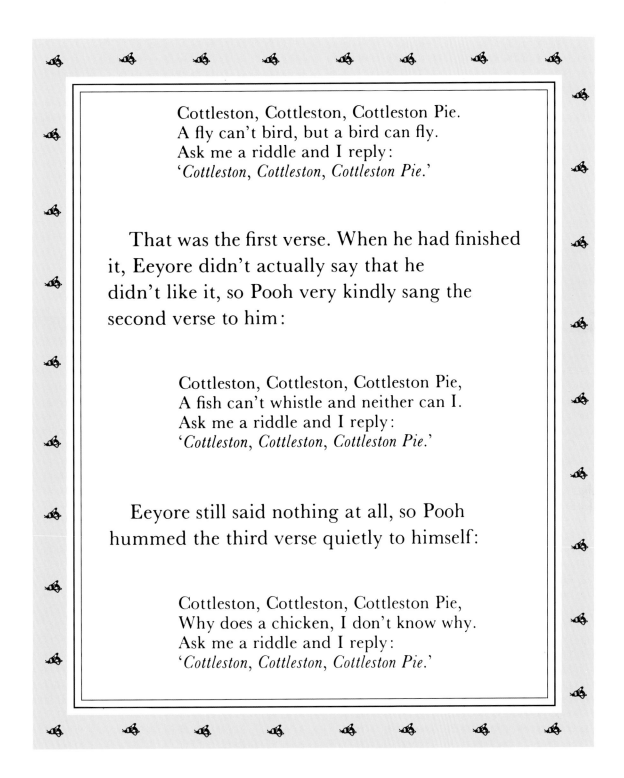

Cottleston, Cottleston, Cottleston Pie.
A fly can't bird, but a bird can fly.
Ask me a riddle and I reply:
'*Cottleston, Cottleston, Cottleston Pie.*'

That was the first verse. When he had finished it, Eeyore didn't actually say that he didn't like it, so Pooh very kindly sang the second verse to him:

Cottleston, Cottleston, Cottleston Pie,
A fish can't whistle and neither can I.
Ask me a riddle and I reply:
'*Cottleston, Cottleston, Cottleston Pie.*'

Eeyore still said nothing at all, so Pooh hummed the third verse quietly to himself:

Cottleston, Cottleston, Cottleston Pie,
Why does a chicken, I don't know why.
Ask me a riddle and I reply:
'*Cottleston, Cottleston, Cottleston Pie.*'

'That's right,' said Eeyore. 'Sing. Umty-tiddly, umty-too. Here we go gathering Nuts and May. Enjoy yourself.'

'I am,' said Pooh.

'Some can,' said Eeyore.

'Why, what's the matter?'

'*Is* anything the matter?'

'You seem so sad, Eeyore.'

'Sad? Why should I be sad? It's my birthday. The happiest day of the year.'

'Your birthday?' said Pooh in great surprise.

'Of course it is. Can't you see? Look at all the presents I have had.' He waved a foot from side to side. 'Look at the birthday cake. Candles and pink sugar.'

Pooh looked – first to the right and then to the left.

'Presents?' said Pooh. 'Birthday cake?' said Pooh. '*Where?*'

'Can't you see them?'

'No,' said Pooh.

'Neither can I,' said Eeyore. 'Joke,'

he explained. 'Ha ha!'

Pooh scratched his head, being a little puzzled by all this.

'But is it really your birthday?' he asked.

'It is.'

'Oh! Well, many happy returns of the day, Eeyore.'

'And many happy returns to you, Pooh Bear.'

'But it isn't *my* birthday.'

'No, it's mine.'

'But you said "Many happy returns"—'

'Well, why not? You don't always want to be miserable on my birthday, do you?'

'Oh, I see,' said Pooh.

'It's bad enough,' said Eeyore, almost breaking down, 'being miserable myself, what with no presents and no cake and no candles, and no proper notice taken of me at all, but if everybody else is going to be miserable too—'

This was too much for Pooh. 'Stay there!' he called to Eeyore, as he turned and hurried back home as quick as he could; for he felt that he must get poor Eeyore a present of *some* sort at once, and he could always think of a proper one afterwards.

Outside his house he found Piglet, jumping up and down trying to reach the knocker.

'Hallo, Piglet,' he said.

'Hallo, Pooh,' said Piglet.

'What are *you* trying to do?'

'I was trying to reach the knocker,' said Piglet. 'I just came round—'

'Let me do it for you,' said Pooh kindly. So he reached up and knocked at the door. 'I have just seen Eeyore,' he began, 'and poor Eeyore is in a Very Sad Condition,

because it's his birthday, and nobody has
taken any notice of it, and he's very Gloomy –
you know what Eeyore is – and there he was,
and— What a long time whoever lives here is
answering this door.' And he knocked again.

'But, Pooh,' said Piglet, 'it's your own house!'

'Oh!' said Pooh. 'So it is,' he said. 'Well,
let's go in.'

So in they went. The first thing Pooh did was

to go to the cupboard to see if he had quite a small jar of honey left; and he had, so he took it down.

'I'm giving this to Eeyore,' he explained, 'as a present. What are *you* going to give?'

'Couldn't I give it too?' said Piglet. 'From both of us?'

'No,' said Pooh. 'That would *not* be a good plan.'

'All right, then, I'll give him a balloon. I've got one left from my party. I'll go and get it now, shall I?'

'That, Piglet, is a *very* good idea. It is just what Eeyore wants to cheer him up. Nobody can be uncheered with a balloon.'

So off Piglet trotted; and in the other direction went Pooh, with his jar of honey.

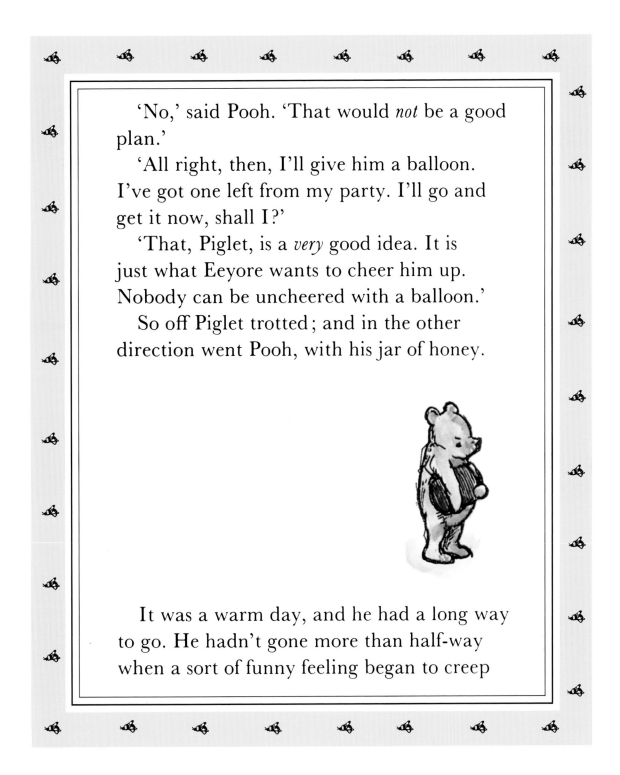

It was a warm day, and he had a long way to go. He hadn't gone more than half-way when a sort of funny feeling began to creep

all over him. It began at the tip of his
nose and trickled all through him and out
at the soles of his feet. It was just as if

somebody inside him were saying, 'Now
then, Pooh, time for a little something.'

'Dear, dear,' said Pooh, 'I didn't know it
was as late as that.' So he sat down and
took the top off his jar of honey. 'Lucky I
brought this with me,' he thought. 'Many
a bear going out on a warm day like this
would never have thought of bringing
a little something with him.'

And he began to eat.

'Now let me see,' he thought, as he took

his last lick of the inside of the jar, 'where was I going? Ah, yes, Eeyore.' He got up slowly.

And then, suddenly, he remembered. He had eaten Eeyore's birthday present!

'*Bother*!' said Pooh. 'What *shall* I do? I *must* give him *something*.'

For a little while he couldn't think of any thing. Then he thought: 'Well, it's a very nice pot, even if there's no honey in it, and if I washed it clean, and got somebody to write '*A Happy Birthday*' on it, Eeyore could keep things in it, which might be Useful.' So, as he was just passing the Hundred Acre Wood, he went inside to call on Owl, who lived there.

'Good morning, Pooh,' said Owl.

'Good morning, Owl,' he said.

'Many happy returns of Eeyore's birthday,' said Pooh.

'Oh, is that what it is?'

'What are you giving him, Owl?'

'What are *you* giving him, Pooh?'

'I'm giving him a Useful Pot to Keep Things In, and I wanted to ask you—'

'Is this it?' said Owl, taking it out of Pooh's paw.

'Yes, and I wanted to ask you—'

'Somebody has been keeping honey in it,' said Owl.

'You can keep *anything* in it,' said Pooh earnestly. 'It's Very Useful like that. And I wanted to ask you—'

'You ought to write "A Happy Birthday" on it.'

'*That* was what I wanted to ask you,' said Pooh. 'Because my spelling is Wobbly. It's good spelling but it Wobbles, and the letters get in the wrong places. Would *you* write "A Happy Birthday" on it for me?'

'It's a nice pot,' said Owl, looking at it all round. 'Couldn't I give it too? From both of us?'

'No,' said Pooh. 'That would *not* be a good plan. Now I'll just wash it first, and then you can write on it.'

Well, he washed the pot out, and dried it, while Owl licked the end of his pencil, and wondered how to spell 'birthday'.

'Can you read, Pooh?' he asked a little anxiously. 'There's a notice about knocking and ringing outside my door, which Christopher Robin wrote. Could you read it?'

'Christopher Robin told me what it said, and *then* I could.'

'Well, I'll tell you what *this* says, and then you'll be able to.'

So Owl wrote . . . and this is what he wrote:
HIPY PAPY BTHUTHDTH
THUTHDA BTHUTHDY.

Pooh looked on admiringly.

'I'm just saying "A Happy Birthday",' said Owl carelessly.

'It's a nice long one,' said Pooh, very much impressed by it.

'Well, *actually*, of course, I'm saying "A Very Happy Birthday with love from Pooh." Naturally it takes a good deal of pencil to say a long thing like that.'

'Oh, I see,' said Pooh.

While all this was happening, Piglet had gone back to his own house to get Eeyore's balloon. He held it very tightly against himself, so that it shouldn't blow away, and he

ran as fast as he could so as to get to

Eeyore before Pooh did; for he thought
that he would like to be the first one to give
a present, just as if he had thought of it
without being told by anybody. And running along, and thinking how pleased
Eeyore would be, he didn't look where he
was going . . . and suddenly he put his foot

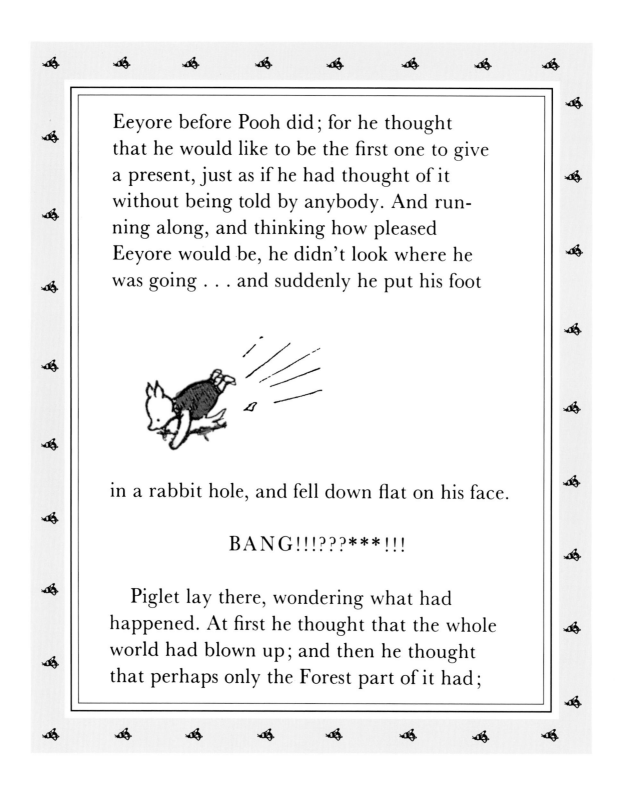

in a rabbit hole, and fell down flat on his face.

BANG!!!???***!!!

Piglet lay there, wondering what had
happened. At first he thought that the whole
world had blown up; and then he thought
that perhaps only the Forest part of it had;

and then he thought that perhaps only *he* had, and he was now alone in the moon or somewhere, and would never see Christopher Robin or Pooh or Eeyore again. And then he thought, 'Well, even if I'm in the moon, I needn't be face downwards all the time,' so he got cautiously up and looked about him.

He was still in the Forest!

'Well, that's funny,' he thought. 'I wonder what that bang was. I couldn't have made such a noise just falling down. And where's my balloon? And what's that small piece of damp rag doing?'

It was the balloon!

'Oh, dear!' said Piglet. 'Oh, dear, oh, dearie, dearie, dear! Well, it's too late now. I can't go back, and I haven't another balloon, and perhaps Eeyore doesn't *like* balloons so *very* much.'

So he trotted on, rather sadly now, and down he came to the side of the stream where Eeyore was, and called out to him.

'Good morning, Eeyore,' shouted Piglet.
'Good morning, Little Piglet,' said Eeyore.

'If it *is* a good morning,' he said. 'Which I doubt,' said he. 'Not that it matters,' he said.

'Many happy returns of the day,' said Piglet, having now got closer.

Eeyore stopped looking at himself in the stream, and turned to stare at Piglet.

'Just say that again,' he said.

'Many hap—'

'Wait a moment.'

Balancing on three legs, he began to bring his fourth leg very cautiously up to his ear.

'I did this yesterday,' he explained, as he fell down for the third time. 'It's quite easy. It's so as I can hear better. . . . There, that's done it! Now then, what were you saying?' He pushed his ear forward with his hoof.

'Many happy returns of the day,' said Piglet again.

'Meaning me?'

'Of course, Eeyore.'

'My birthday?'

'Yes.'

'Me having a real birthday?'

'Yes, Eeyore, and I've brought you a present.'

Eeyore took down his right hoof from his right ear, turned round, and with great difficulty put up his left hoof.

'I must have that in the other ear,' he said. 'Now then.'

'A present,' said Piglet very loudly.

'Meaning me again?'

'Yes.'

'My birthday still?'

'Of course, Eeyore.'

'Me going on having a real birthday?'

'Yes, Eeyore, and I brought you a balloon.'

'*Balloon?*' said Eeyore. 'You did say balloon? One of those big coloured things you blow up? Gaiety, song-and-dance, here we are and there we are?'

'Yes, but I'm afraid – I'm very sorry, Eeyore – but when I was running along to bring it to you, I fell down.'

'Dear, dear, how unlucky! You ran too fast, I expect. You didn't hurt yourself, Little Piglet?'

'No, but I – I – oh, Eeyore, I burst the balloon!'

'My balloon?' said Eeyore at last.
'My birthday balloon?'
Piglet nodded.
There was a very long silence.

'Yes, Eeyore,' said Piglet, sniffing a little.

'Here it is. With – with many happy returns of the day.' And he gave Eeyore the small piece of damp rag.

'Is this it?' said Eeyore, a little surprised.

Piglet nodded.

'My present?'

Piglet nodded again.

'The balloon?'

'Yes.'

'Thank you, Piglet,' said Eeyore. 'You don't mind my asking,' he went on, 'but what colour was this balloon when it – when it *was* a balloon?'

'Red.'

'I just wondered. . . . Red,' he murmured to himself. 'My favourite colour. . . . How big was it?'

'About as big as me.'

'I just wondered. . . . About as big as Piglet,' he said to himself sadly. 'My favourite size. Well, well.'

Piglet felt very miserable, and didn't know
what to say. He was still opening his mouth
to begin something, and then deciding that it
wasn't any good saying *that*, when he heard
a shout from the other side of the river, and

there was Pooh.

'Many happy returns of the day,' called
out Pooh, forgetting that he had said it
already.

'Thank you, Pooh, I'm having them,' said
Eeyore gloomily.

'I've brought you a little present,' said Pooh excitedly.

'I've had it,' said Eeyore.

Pooh had now splashed across the stream to Eeyore, and Piglet was sitting a little way off, his head in his paws, snuffling to himself.

'It's a Useful Pot,' said Pooh. 'Here it is. And it's got "A Very Happy Birthday with love from Pooh" written on it. That's what all that writing is. And it's for putting things in. There!'

When Eeyore saw the pot, he became quite excited.

'Why!' he said. 'I believe my Balloon will just go into that Pot!'

'Oh, no, Eeyore,' said Pooh. 'Balloons are much too big to go into Pots. What you do with a balloon is, you hold the balloon—'

'Not mine,' said Eeyore proudly. 'Look, Piglet!' And as Piglet looked sorrowfully round, Eeyore picked the balloon up with his teeth, and placed it carefully in the pot; picked it out and put it on the ground; and then picked it up again and put it carefully back.

'So it does!' said Pooh. 'It goes in!'

'So it does!' said Piglet. 'And it comes out!'

'Doesn't it?' said Eeyore. 'It goes in and out like anything.'

'I'm very glad,' said Pooh happily, 'that I thought of giving you a Useful Pot to put things in.'

'I'm very glad,' said Piglet happily, 'that I thought of giving you Something to put in a Useful Pot.'

But Eeyore wasn't listening. He was taking the balloon out, and putting it back again, as happy as could be. . . .

'And didn't *I* give him anything?' asked Christopher Robin sadly.

'Of course you did,' I said. 'You gave him – don't you remember – a little – a little—'

'I gave him a box of paints to paint things with.'

'That was it.'

'Why didn't I give it to him in the morning?'

'You were so busy getting his party ready for him. He had a cake with icing on the top, and three candles, and his name in pink sugar, and—'

'Yes, *I* remember,' said Christopher Robin.

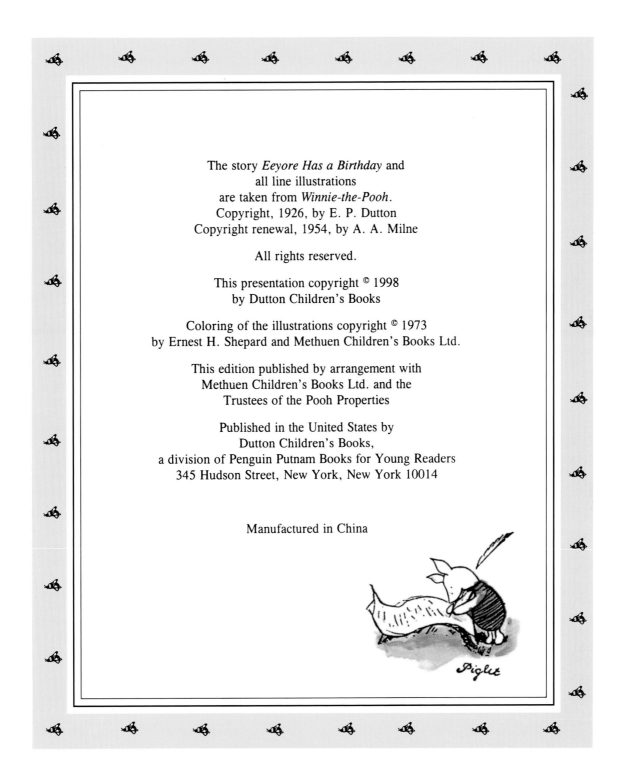

157

Pooh

158

A. A. MILNE

Piglet Is Entirely Surrounded by Water

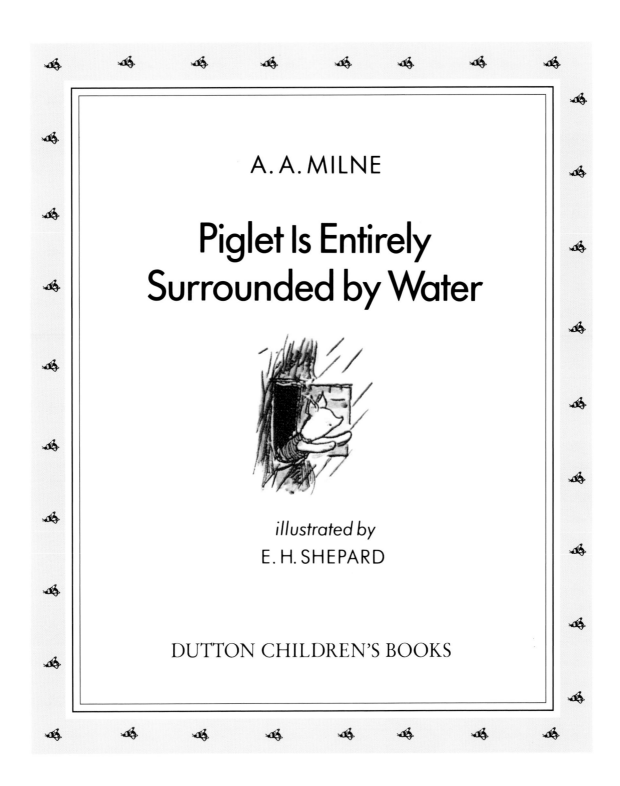

illustrated by

E. H. SHEPARD

DUTTON CHILDREN'S BOOKS

Piglet Is Entirely Surrounded by Water

It rained and it rained and it rained.
Piglet told himself that never in all
his life, and *he* was goodness knows *how*
old – three, was it, or four? – never
had he seen so much rain. Days and days
and days.

'If only,' he thought, as he looked
out of the window, 'I had been in Pooh's

house, or Christopher Robin's house, or Rabbit's house when it began to rain, then I should have had Company all this time, instead of being here all alone, with nothing to do except wonder when it will stop.' And he imagined himself with Pooh, saying, 'Did you ever see such rain, Pooh?' and Pooh saying, 'Isn't it *awful*, Piglet?' and Piglet saying, 'I wonder how it is over Christopher Robin's way,' and Pooh saying, 'I should think poor old Rabbit is about flooded out by this time.' It would have been jolly to talk like this, and really, it wasn't much good having anything exciting like floods, if you couldn't share them with somebody.

For it was rather exciting. The little dry ditches in which Piglet had nosed about so often had become streams, the little streams across which he had splashed were rivers, and the river, between whose steep banks they had played so happily, had sprawled out of its own bed and was taking up so much room everywhere, that Piglet was beginning to wonder whether it would be coming into *his* bed soon.

'It's a little Anxious,' he said to himself, 'to be a Very Small Animal Entirely Surrounded by Water. Christopher Robin and Pooh could escape by Climbing Trees, and Kanga could escape by Jumping, and Rabbit could escape by Burrowing, and Owl could escape by Flying, and Eeyore could escape by – by Making a Loud Noise Until Rescued, and here am I, surrounded by water and I can't do *anything*.'

It went on raining, and every day the water got a little higher, until now it was nearly up to Piglet's window . . . and still he hadn't done anything.

'There's Pooh,' he thought to himself. 'Pooh hasn't much Brain, but he never comes to any harm. He does silly things and they turn out right. There's Owl. Owl hasn't exactly got Brain, but he Knows Things. He would know the Right Thing to do when Surrounded by Water. There's Rabbit. He hasn't Learnt in Books, but he can always Think of a Clever Plan. There's Kanga. She isn't Clever, Kanga isn't, but she would be so anxious about Roo that she would do a Good Thing to do without thinking about it. And then there's Eeyore. And Eeyore is so miserable anyhow that he wouldn't mind about this. But I wonder what Christopher Robin would do?'

Then suddenly he remembered a story which Christopher Robin had told him about a man on a

desert island who had written something
in a bottle and thrown it into the sea;
and Piglet thought that if he wrote something
in a bottle and threw it in the water,
perhaps somebody would come and rescue *him*!

He left the window and began to search
his house, all of it that wasn't under
water, and at last he found a pencil and
a small piece of dry paper, and a bottle
with a cork to it. And he wrote on one
side of the paper:

HELP!
PIGLET (ME)

and on the other side:

IT'S ME PIGLET, HELP HELP.

Then he put the paper in the bottle,
and he corked the bottle up as tightly as
he could, and he leant out of his window as
far as he could lean without falling in,
and he threw the bottle as far as he could

throw – *splash!* – and in a little while it
bobbed up again on the water; and he
watched it floating slowly away in the distance,
until his eyes ached with looking,

and sometimes he thought it was the bottle,
and sometimes he thought it was just a ripple
on the water which he was following, and
then suddenly he knew that he would never
see it again and that he had done all that
he could do to save himself.

'So now,' he thought, 'somebody else
will have to do something, and I hope they
will do it soon, because if they don't I
shall have to swim, which I can't, so I
hope they do it soon.' And then he gave a

very long sigh and said, 'I wish Pooh were
here. It's so much more friendly
with two.'

When the rain began Pooh was asleep.
It rained, and it rained, and it rained,
and he slept and he slept and he slept.
He had had a tiring day. You remember how
he discovered the North Pole; well, he
was so proud of this that he asked Christopher
Robin if there were any other Poles such as
a Bear of Little Brain might discover.

'There's a South Pole,' said Christopher
Robin, 'and I expect there's an East
Pole and a West Pole, though people

don't like talking about them.'

Pooh was very excited when he heard this, and suggested that they should have an Expotition to discover the East Pole, but Christopher Robin had thought of something else to do with Kanga; so Pooh went out to discover the East Pole by himself. Whether he discovered it or not, I forget; but he was so tired when he got home that, in the very middle of his supper, after he had been eating for little more than half-an-hour, he fell fast asleep in his chair, and slept and slept and slept.

Then suddenly he was dreaming. He was at the East Pole, and it was a very cold pole with the coldest sort of snow and ice all over it. He had found a beehive to sleep in, but there wasn't room for his legs, so he had left them outside. And Wild Woozles, such as inhabit the East Pole, came and nibbled all the fur off his legs to make Nests for their Young. And the

more they nibbled, the colder his legs
got, until suddenly he woke up with an
Ow! – and there he was, sitting in his
chair with his feet in the water, and
water all round him!

He splashed to his door and looked out. . . .

'This is Serious,' said Pooh. 'I must
have an Escape.'

So he took his largest pot of honey
and escaped with it to a broad branch of
his tree, well above the water, and then
he climbed down again and escaped with
another pot . . . and when the whole Escape
was finished, there was Pooh sitting on
his branch, dangling his legs, and there,
beside him, were ten pots of honey. . . .

Two days later, there was Pooh, sitting
on his branch, dangling his legs, and there,
beside him, was one pot of honey.

Four days later, there was Pooh. . . .

And it was on the morning of the fourth
day that Piglet's bottle came floating past

him, and with one loud cry of 'Honey!'
Pooh plunged into the water, seized the
bottle, and struggled back to his tree
again.

'Bother!' said Pooh, as he opened it.
'All that wet for nothing. What's that bit
of paper doing?'

He took it out and looked at it.

'It's a Missage,' he said to himself,

'that's what it is. And that letter is a "P", and so is that, and so is that, and "P" means "Pooh", so it's a very important Missage to me, and I can't read it. I must find Christopher Robin or Owl or Piglet, one of those Clever Readers who can read things, and they will tell me what this missage means. Only I can't swim. Bother!'

Then he had an idea, and I think that for a Bear of Very Little Brain, it was a good idea. He said to himself:

'If a bottle can float, then a jar can float, and if a jar floats, I can sit on the top of it, if it's a very big jar.'

So he took his biggest jar, and corked it up.

'All boats have to have a name,' he said, 'so I shall call mine *The Floating Bear*.' And with these words he dropped his boat into the water and jumped in after it.

For a little while Pooh and *The Floating Bear*
were uncertain as to which of them
was meant to be on the top, but after trying

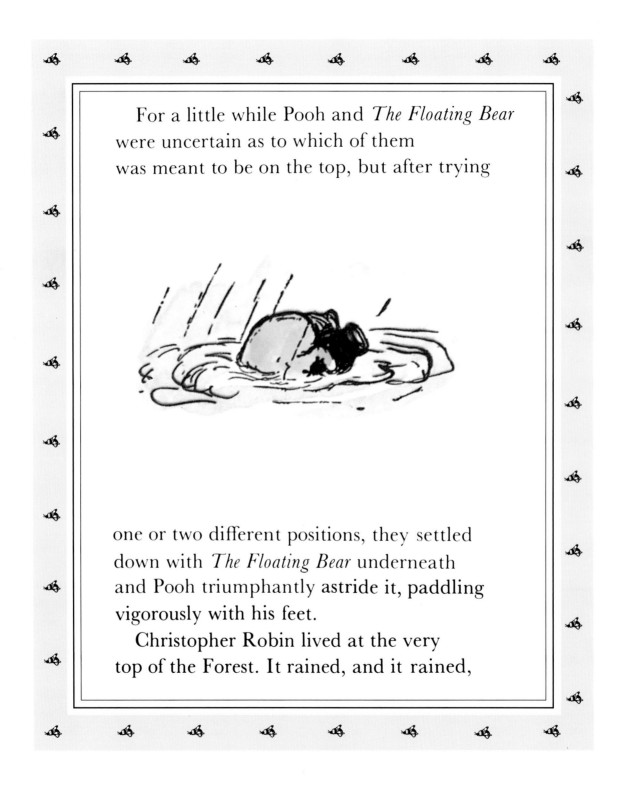

one or two different positions, they settled
down with *The Floating Bear* underneath
and Pooh triumphantly astride it, paddling
vigorously with his feet.

Christopher Robin lived at the very
top of the Forest. It rained, and it rained,

and it rained, but the water
couldn't come up to *his* house. It was
rather jolly to look down into the valleys
and see the water all round him, but it
rained so hard that he stayed indoors most
of the time, and thought about things.
Every morning he went out with his umbrella
and put a stick in the place where the
water came up to, and every next morning
he went out and couldn't see his stick
any more, so he put another stick in the
place where the water came up to, and then
he walked home again, and each morning he

had a shorter walk to walk than he had had the morning before. On the morning of the fifth day he saw the water all round him, and knew that for the first time in his life he was on a real island. Which was very exciting.

It was on this morning that Owl came flying over the water to say 'How do you do?' to his friend Christopher Robin.

'I say, Owl,' said Christopher Robin, 'isn't this fun? I'm on an island.'

'The atmospheric conditions have been very unfavourable lately,' said Owl.

'The what?'

'It has been raining,' explained Owl.

'Yes.' said Christopher Robin. 'It has.'

'The flood-level has reached an unprecedented height.'

'The who?'

'There's a lot of water about,' explained Owl.

'Yes,' said Christopher Robin,
'there is.'
    'However, the prospects are rapidly
becoming more favourable. At any moment—'

'Have you seen Pooh?'

'No. At any moment—'

'I hope he's all right,' said Christopher Robin. 'I've been wondering about him. I expect Piglet's with him. Do you think they're all right, Owl?'

'I expect so. You see, at any moment—'

'Do go and see, Owl. Because Pooh hasn't got very much brain, and he might do something silly, and I do love him so, Owl. Do you see, Owl?'

'That's all right,' said Owl. 'I'll go. Back directly.' And he flew off.

In a little while he was back again.

'Pooh isn't there,' he said.

'Not there?'

'He's *been* there. He's been sitting on a branch of his tree outside his house with nine pots of honey. But he isn't there now.'

'Oh, Pooh!' cried Christopher Robin. 'Where *are* you?'

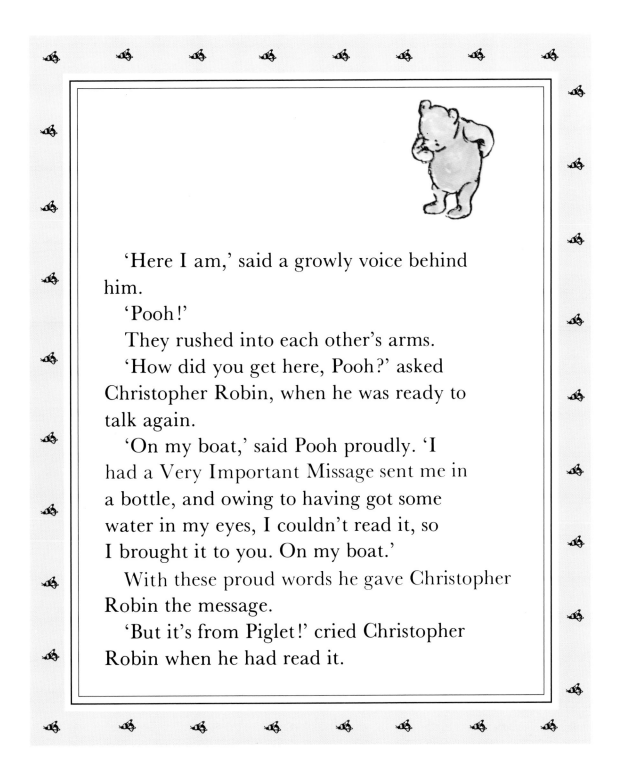

'Here I am,' said a growly voice behind
him.

'Pooh!'

They rushed into each other's arms.

'How did you get here, Pooh?' asked
Christopher Robin, when he was ready to
talk again.

'On my boat,' said Pooh proudly. 'I
had a Very Important Missage sent me in
a bottle, and owing to having got some
water in my eyes, I couldn't read it, so
I brought it to you. On my boat.'

With these proud words he gave Christopher
Robin the message.

'But it's from Piglet!' cried Christopher
Robin when he had read it.

'Isn't there anything about Pooh in it?'
asked Bear, looking over his shoulder.

Christopher Robin read the message
aloud.

'Oh, are those "P's" piglets? I
thought they were poohs.'

'We must rescue him at once! I thought
he was with *you*, Pooh. Owl, could you rescue
him on your back?'

'I don't think so,' said Owl, after grave
thought. 'It is doubtful if the necessary
dorsal muscles—'

'Then would you fly to him at *once* and
say that Rescue is Coming? And Pooh
and I will think of a Rescue and come as
quick as ever we can. Oh, don't *talk*,
Owl, go on quick!' And, still thinking
of something to say, Owl flew off.

'Now then, Pooh,' said Christopher
Robin, 'where's your boat?'

'I ought to say,' explained Pooh as
they walked down to the shore of the

island, 'that it isn't just an ordinary
sort of boat. Sometimes it's a Boat,
and sometimes it's more of an Accident.
It all depends.'

'Depends on what?'

'On whether I'm on the top of it or
underneath it.'

'Oh! Well, where is it?'

'There!' said Pooh, pointing proudly to
The Floating Bear.

It wasn't what Christopher Robin
expected, and the more he looked at it, the
more he thought what a Brave and Clever

Bear Pooh was, and the more Christopher Robin thought this, the more Pooh looked modestly down his nose and tried to pretend he wasn't.

'But it's too small for two of us,' said Christopher Robin sadly.

'Three of us with Piglet.'

'That makes it smaller still. Oh, Pooh Bear, what shall we do?'

And then this Bear, Pooh Bear, Winnie-the-Pooh, F.O.P. (Friend of Piglet's), R.C. (Rabbit's Companion), P.D. (Pole Discoverer), E.C. and T.F. (Eeyore's Comforter and Tail-Finder) – in fact, Pooh himself – said something so clever that Christopher Robin could only look at him with mouth open and eyes staring, wondering if this was really the Bear of Very Little Brain whom he had known and loved so long.

'We might go in your umbrella,' said Pooh.

'?'

'We might go in your umbrella,'
said Pooh.

'??'

'We might go in your umbrella,'
said Pooh.

'!!!!!!'

For suddenly Christopher Robin saw that they might. He opened his umbrella and put it point downwards in the water. It floated but wobbled. Pooh got in. He was just beginning to say that it was all right now, when he found that it

wasn't, so after a short drink, which he didn't really want, he waded back to Christopher Robin. Then they both got in together, and it wobbled no longer.

'I shall call this boat *The Brain of Pooh*,' said Christopher Robin, and *The Brain of Pooh* set sail forthwith in a south-westerly direction, revolving gracefully.

You can imagine Piglet's joy when at last the ship came in sight of him. In after-years he liked to think that he had been in Very Great Danger during the Terrible Flood, but the only danger he had really been in was the last half-hour of his imprisonment, when Owl, who had just flown up, sat on a branch of his tree to comfort him, and told him a very long story about an aunt who had once laid a seagull's egg by mistake, and the story went on and on, rather like this sentence, until Piglet who was listening out of his

window without much hope, went to sleep
quietly and naturally, slipping slowly
out of the window towards the water
until he was only hanging on by his toes,
at which moment, luckily, a sudden loud
squawk from Owl, which was really part
of the story, being what his aunt said,
woke the Piglet up and just gave him time

to jerk himself back into safety and say, 'How interesting, and did she?' when – well, you can imagine his joy when at last he saw the good ship, *Brain of Pooh* (*Captain*, C. Robin: *1st Mate*, P. Bear) coming over the sea to rescue him. . . .

And as that is really the end of the story, and I am very tired after that last sentence, I think I shall stop there.

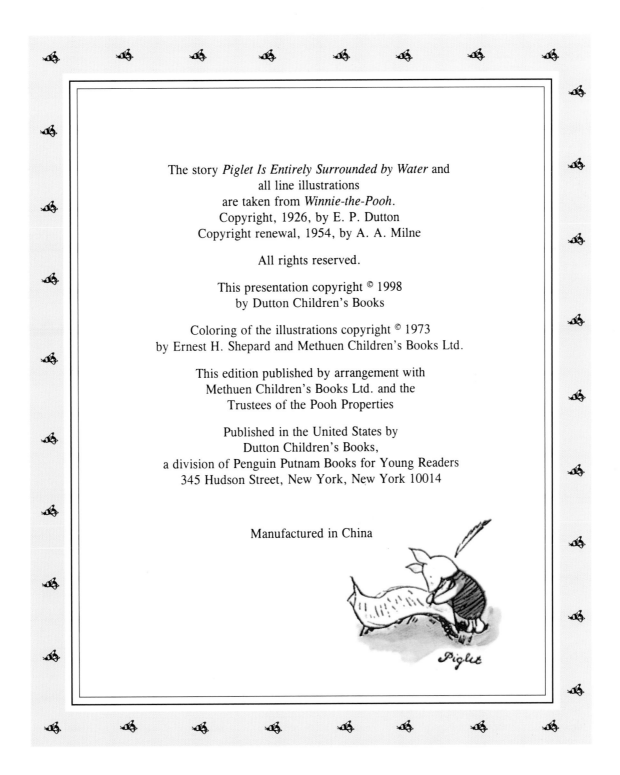

A. A. MILNE

An Expotition to the North Pole

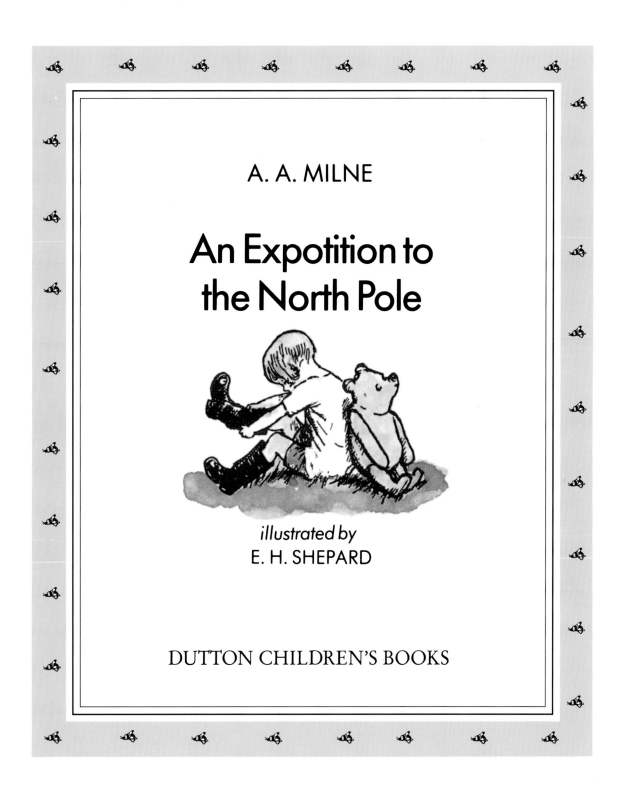

illustrated by
E. H. SHEPARD

DUTTON CHILDREN'S BOOKS

One fine day Pooh had stumped up to the top of the Forest to see if his friend Christopher Robin was interested in Bears at all. At breakfast that morning (a simple meal of marmalade spread lightly over a honeycomb or two) he had suddenly thought of a new song. It began like this:

'Sing Ho! for the life of a Bear.'

When he had got as far as this, he scratched his head, and thought to himself,

'That's a very good start for a song, but what about the second line?' He tried sing-ing 'Ho,' two or three times, but it didn't  seem to help. 'Perhaps it would be better,' he thought, 'if I sang Hi for the life of a Bear.' So he sang it . . . but it wasn't.

'Very well, then,' he said, 'I shall sing
that first line twice, and perhaps if I sing
it very quickly, I shall find myself singing
the third and fourth lines before I have
time to think of them, and that will be a
Good Song. Now then:

Sing Ho! for the life of a Bear!
Sing Ho! for the life of a Bear!
I don't much mind if it rains or snows,
'Cos I've got a lot of honey on my nice new nose!
I don't much care if it snows or thaws,
'Cos I've got a lot of honey on my nice clean paws!
Sing Ho! for a Bear!
Sing Ho! for a Pooh!
And I'll have a little something in an hour or two!'

He was so pleased with this song that
he sang it all the way to the top of the
Forest, 'and if I go on singing it much
longer,' he thought, 'it will be time for
the little something, and then the last

line won't be true.' So he turned it into
a hum instead.

Christopher Robin was sitting outside
his door, putting on his Big Boots. As soon
as he saw the Big Boots, Pooh knew that an
Adventure was going to happen, and he brushed
the honey off his nose with the back of his
paw, and spruced himself up as well as he
could, so as to look Ready for Anything.

'Good morning, Christopher Robin,' he
called out.

'Hallo, Pooh Bear. I can't get this
boot on.'

'That's bad,' said Pooh.

'Do you think you could very kindly lean
against me, 'cos I keep pulling so hard
that I fall over backwards.'

Pooh sat down, dug his feet into the
ground, and pushed hard against Christopher
Robin's back, and Christopher Robin pushed
hard against his, and pulled and pulled at
his boot until he had got it on.

'And that's that,' said Pooh. 'What do we do next?'

'We are all going on an Expedition,' said Christopher Robin, as he got up and brushed himself. 'Thank you, Pooh.'

'Going on an Expotition?' said Pooh eagerly. 'I don't think I've ever been on one of those. Where are we going to on this Expotition?'

'Expedition, silly old Bear. It's got an "x" in it.'

'Oh!' said Pooh. 'I know.' But he didn't really.

'We're going to discover the North Pole.'

'Oh!' said Pooh again. 'What *is* the North Pole?' he asked.

'It's just a thing you discover,' said Christopher Robin carelessly, not being quite sure himself.

'Oh! I see,' said Pooh. 'Are bears any good at discovering it?'

'Of course they are. And Rabbit and Kanga and all of you. It's an Expedition. That's what an Expedition means. A long line of everybody. You'd better tell the others to get ready, while I see if my gun's all right. And we must all bring Provisions.'

'Bring what?'

'Things to eat.'

'Oh!' said Pooh happily. 'I thought you said Provisions. I'll go and tell them.' And he stumped off.

The first person he met was Rabbit.

'Hallo, Rabbit,' he said, 'is that you?'

'Let's pretend it isn't,' said Rabbit, 'and see what happens.'

'I've got a message for you.'

'I'll give it to him.'

'We're all going on an Expotition with Christopher Robin!'

'What is it when we're on it?'

'A sort of boat, I think,' said Pooh.

'Oh! that sort.'

'Yes. And we're going to discover
a Pole or something. Or was it a
Mole? Anyhow we're going to discover it.'

'We are, are we?' said Rabbit.

'Yes. And we've got to bring Pro—
things to eat with us. In case we want
to eat them. Now I'm going down to
Piglet's. Tell Kanga, will you?'

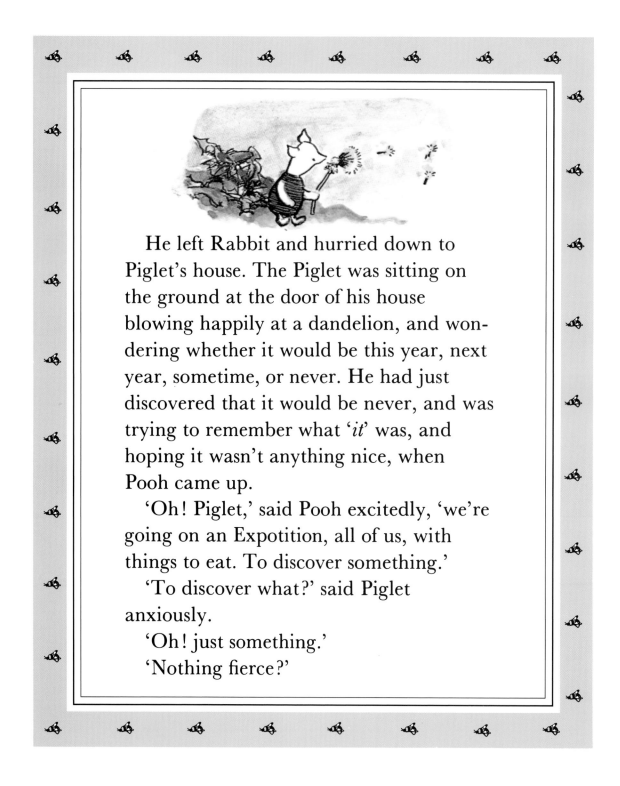

He left Rabbit and hurried down to
Piglet's house. The Piglet was sitting on
the ground at the door of his house
blowing happily at a dandelion, and wondering whether it would be this year, next
year, sometime, or never. He had just
discovered that it would be never, and was
trying to remember what '*it*' was, and
hoping it wasn't anything nice, when
Pooh came up.

'Oh! Piglet,' said Pooh excitedly, 'we're
going on an Expotition, all of us, with
things to eat. To discover something.'

'To discover what?' said Piglet
anxiously.

'Oh! just something.'

'Nothing fierce?'

'Christopher Robin didn't say anything about fierce. He just said it had an "x".'

'It isn't their necks I mind,' said Piglet earnestly. 'It's their teeth. But if Christopher Robin is coming I don't mind anything.'

In a little while they were all ready at the top of the Forest, and the Expotition started. First came Christopher Robin and Rabbit, then Piglet and Pooh; then Kanga, with Roo in her pocket, and Owl; then Eeyore; and, at the end, in a long line, all Rabbit's friends-and-relations.

'I didn't ask them,' explained Rabbit carelessly. 'They just came. They always

do. They can march at the end, after Eeyore.'

'What I say,' said Eeyore, 'is that it's unsettling. I didn't want to come on this Expo – what Pooh said. I only came to oblige. But here I am; and if I am the end of the Expo – what we're talking about – then let me *be* the end. But if, every time I want to sit down for a little rest, I have to brush away half a dozen of Rabbit's smaller.friends-and-relations first, then this isn't an Expo – whatever it is – at all, it's simply a Confused Noise. That's what *I* say.'

'I see what Eeyore means,' said Owl. 'If you ask me—'

'I'm not asking anybody,' said Eeyore. 'I'm just telling everybody. We can look for the North Pole, or we can play "Here we go gathering Nuts and May" with the end part of an ants' nest. It's all the same to me.'

There was a shout from the top of the line.

'Come on!' called Christopher Robin.

'Come on!' called Pooh and Piglet.

'Come on!' called Owl.

'We're starting,' said Rabbit. 'I must go.' And he hurried off to the front of the Expotition with Christopher Robin.

'All right,' said Eeyore. 'We're going. Only Don't Blame Me.'

So off they all went to discover the

Pole. And as they walked, they chattered to each other of this and that, all except Pooh, who was making up a song.

'This is the first verse,' he said to Piglet, when he was ready with it.

'First verse of what?'

'My song.'

'What song?'

'This one.'

'Which one?'

'Well, if you listen, Piglet, you'll hear it.'

'How do you know I'm not listening?'

Pooh couldn't answer that one, so he began to sing.

> They all went off to discover the Pole,
>   Owl and Piglet and Rabbit and all;
> It's a Thing you Discover, as I've been tole
>   By Owl and Piglet and Rabbit and all.
> Eeyore, Christopher Robin and Pooh
> And Rabbit's relations all went too –
> And where the Pole was none of them knew. . . .
>   Sing Hey! for Owl and Rabbit and all!

'Hush!' said Christopher Robin, turning
round to Pooh, 'we're just coming to
a Dangerous Place.'

'Hush!' said Pooh, turning round
quickly to Piglet.

'Hush!' said Piglet to Kanga.

'Hush!' said Kanga to Owl, while Roo
said 'Hush!' several times to himself
very quietly.

'Hush!' said Owl to Eeyore.

'*Hush!*' said Eeyore in a terrible voice to all Rabbit's friends-and-relations, and 'Hush!' they said hastily to each other all down the line, until it got to the last one of all. And the last and smallest friend-and-relation was so upset to find that the whole Expotition was saying 'Hush!' to *him*, that he buried himself head downwards in a crack in the ground, and stayed there for two days until the danger was over, and then went home in a great hurry, 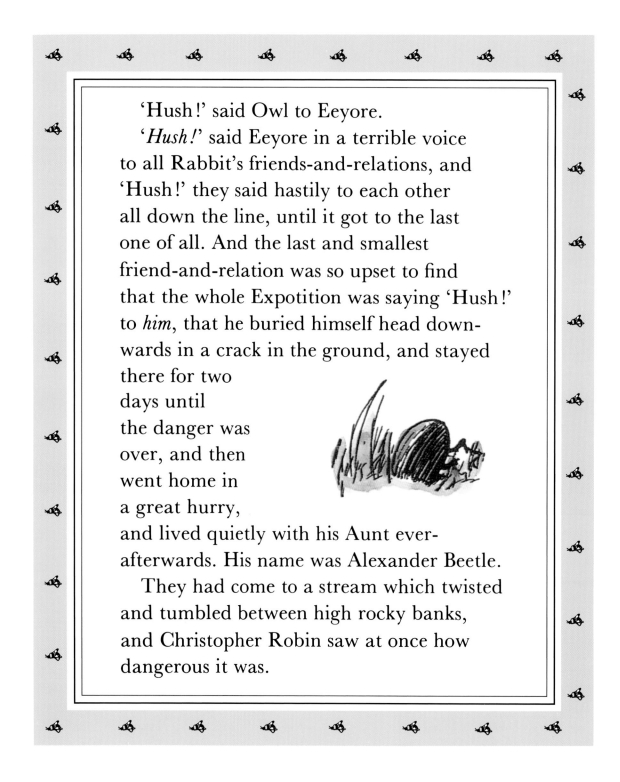 and lived quietly with his Aunt ever-afterwards. His name was Alexander Beetle.

They had come to a stream which twisted and tumbled between high rocky banks, and Christopher Robin saw at once how dangerous it was.

'It's just the place,' he explained, 'for an Ambush.'

'What sort of bush?' whispered Pooh to Piglet. 'A gorse-bush?'

'My dear Pooh,' said Owl in his superior way, 'don't you know what an Ambush is?'

'Owl,' said Piglet, looking round at him severely, 'Pooh's whisper was a perfectly private whisper, and there was no need—'

'An Ambush,' said Owl, 'is a sort of Surprise.'

'So is a gorse-bush sometimes,' said Pooh.

'An Ambush, as I was about to explain to Pooh,' said Piglet, 'is a sort of Surprise.'

'If people jump out at you suddenly, that's an Ambush,' said Owl.

'It's an Ambush, Pooh, when people jump at you suddenly,' explained Piglet.

Pooh, who now knew what an Ambush was, said that a gorse-bush had sprung at him suddenly one day when he fell off a tree, and he had taken six days to get all the prickles out of himself.

'We are not *talking* about gorse-bushes,' said Owl a little crossly.

'I am,' said Pooh.

They were climbing very cautiously up the stream now, going from rock to rock, and after they had gone a little way they came to a place where the banks widened out at each side, so that on each side of the water there was a level strip of grass on which they could sit down and rest. As soon as he saw this, Christopher Robin called 'Halt!' and they all sat down and rested.

'I think,' said Christopher Robin, 'that we ought to eat all our Provisions now, so that we shan't have so much to carry.'

'Eat all our what?' said Pooh.

'All that we've brought,' said Piglet, getting to work.

'That's a good idea,' said Pooh, and he got to work too.

'Have you all got something?' asked Christopher Robin with his mouth full.

'All except me,' said Eeyore. 'As Usual.' He looked round at them in his melancholy way. 'I suppose none of you are sitting on a thistle by any chance?'

'I believe I am,' said Pooh. 'Ow!' He got up, and looked behind him. 'Yes, I was. I thought so.'

'Thank you, Pooh. If you've quite finished with it.' He moved across to Pooh's place, and began to eat.

'It doesn't do them any Good, you know, sitting on them,' he went on, as he looked

up munching. 'Takes all the Life out of them. Remember that another time, all of you. A little Consideration, a little Thought for Others, makes all the difference.'

As soon as he had finished his lunch Christopher Robin whispered to Rabbit, and Rabbit said, 'Yes, yes, of course,' and they walked a little way up the stream together.

'I don't want the others to hear,' said Christopher Robin.

'Quite so,' said Rabbit, looking important.

'It's – I wondered – It's only – Rabbit, I suppose *you* don't know. What does the North Pole *look* like?'

'Well,' said Rabbit, stroking his whiskers. 'Now you're asking me.'

'I did know once, only I've sort of forgotten,' said Christopher Robin carelessly.

'It's a funny thing,' said Rabbit, 'but I've sort of forgotten too, although I did know *once*.'

'I suppose it's just a pole stuck in the ground.'

'Sure to be a pole,' said Rabbit, 'because of calling it a pole, and if it's a pole, well, I should think it would be sticking in the ground, shouldn't you, because there'd be nowhere else to stick it.'

'Yes, that's what I thought.'

'The only thing,' said Rabbit, 'is, *where is it sticking?*'

'That's what we're looking for,' said Christopher Robin.

They went back to the others. Piglet was lying on his back, sleeping peacefully, Roo was washing his face and paws in the stream, while Kanga explained to everybody proudly that this was the first time he had ever washed his face himself, and Owl was telling Kanga an Interesting Anecdote full of long words like Encyclopaedia and Rhododendron to which Kanga wasn't listening.

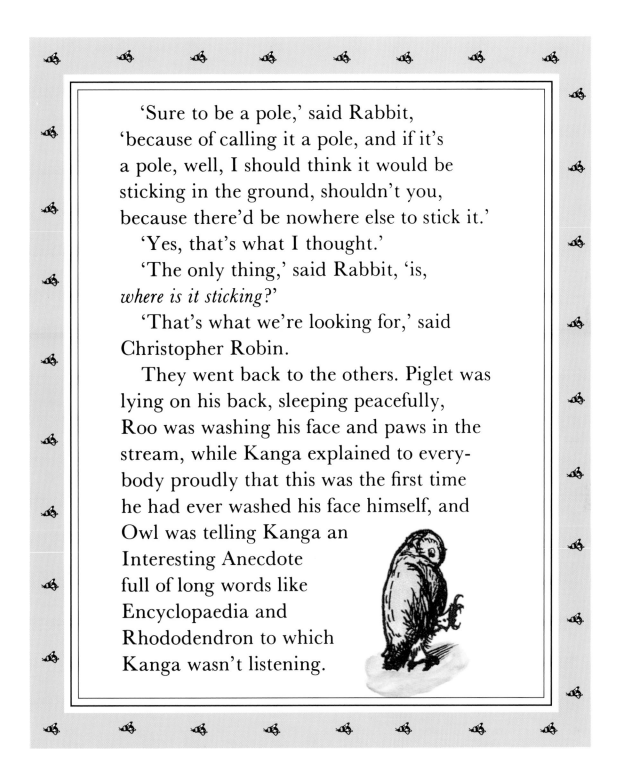

'I don't hold with all this washing,' grumbled Eeyore. 'This modern Behind-the-ears nonsense. What do *you* think, Pooh?'

'Well,' said Pooh, '*I* think—'

But we shall never know what Pooh thought, for there came a sudden squeak from Roo, a splash, and a loud cry of alarm from Kanga.

'So much for *washing*,' said Eeyore.

'Roo's fallen in!' cried Rabbit, and he and Christopher Robin came rushing down to the rescue.

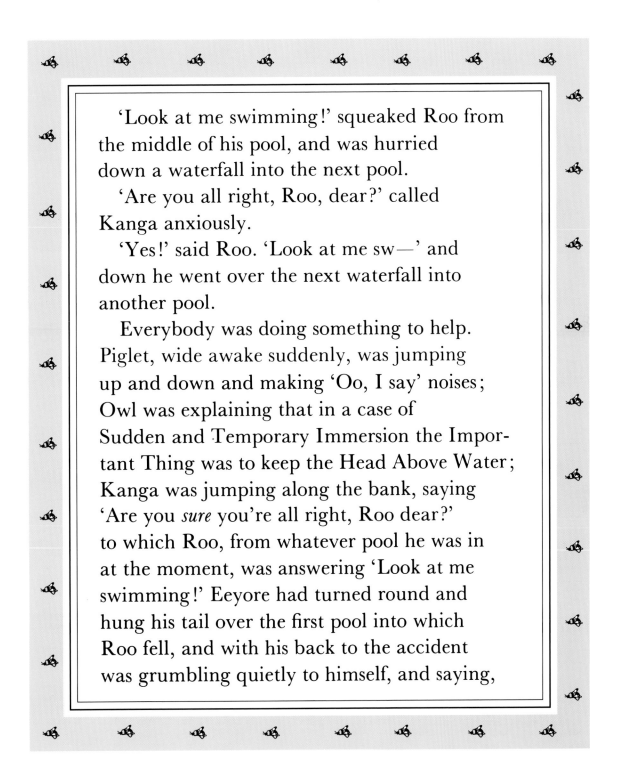

'Look at me swimming!' squeaked Roo from the middle of his pool, and was hurried down a waterfall into the next pool.

'Are you all right, Roo, dear?' called Kanga anxiously.

'Yes!' said Roo. 'Look at me sw—' and down he went over the next waterfall into another pool.

Everybody was doing something to help. Piglet, wide awake suddenly, was jumping up and down and making 'Oo, I say' noises; Owl was explaining that in a case of Sudden and Temporary Immersion the Important Thing was to keep the Head Above Water; Kanga was jumping along the bank, saying 'Are you *sure* you're all right, Roo dear?' to which Roo, from whatever pool he was in at the moment, was answering 'Look at me swimming!' Eeyore had turned round and hung his tail over the first pool into which Roo fell, and with his back to the accident was grumbling quietly to himself, and saying,

'All this washing; but catch on to my tail, little Roo, and you'll be all right'; and Christopher Robin and Rabbit came hurrying past Eeyore, and were calling out to the others in front of them.

'All right, Roo, I'm coming,' called Christopher Robin.

'Get something across the stream, lower down, some of you fellows,' called Rabbit.

But Pooh was getting something. Two pools below Roo he was standing with a long pole in his paws, and Kanga came up and took one end of it, and between them they held it across the lower part of the pool;

and Roo, still bubbling proudly, 'Look at me swimming,' drifted up against it, and climbed out.

'Did you see me swimming?' squeaked Roo excitedly, while Kanga scolded him and rubbed him down. 'Pooh, did you see me swimming? That's called swimming, what I was doing. Rabbit, did you see what I was doing? Swimming. Hallo, Piglet! I say, Piglet! What do you think I was doing! Swimming! Christopher Robin, did you see me—'

But Christopher Robin wasn't listening. He was looking at Pooh.

'Pooh,' he said, 'where did you find that pole?'

Pooh looked at the pole in his hands.

'I just found it,' he said. 'I thought it ought to be useful. I just picked it up.'

'Pooh,' said Christopher Robin solemnly, 'the Expedition is over. You have found the North Pole!'

'Oh!' said Pooh.

Eeyore was sitting with his tail in the water when they all got back to him.

'Tell Roo to be quick, somebody,' he said. 'My tail's getting cold. I don't want to mention it, but I just mention it. I don't want to complain, but there it is. My tail's cold.'

'Here I am!' squeaked Roo.

'Oh, there you are.'

'Did you see me swimming?'

Eeyore took his tail out of the water, and swished it from side to side.

'As I expected,' he said. 'Lost all feeling. Numbed it. That's what it's done. Numbed it. Well, as long as nobody minds, I suppose it's all right.'

'Poor old Eeyore! I'll dry it for you,' said Christopher Robin, and he took out his handkerchief and rubbed it up.

'Thank you, Christopher Robin. You're the only one who seems to understand about tails. They don't think – that's what's the matter with some of these others. They've no imagination. A tail isn't a tail to *them*, it's just a Little Bit Extra at the back.'

'Never mind, Eeyore,' said Christopher Robin, rubbing his hardest. 'Is *that* better?'

'It's feeling more like a tail perhaps. It belongs again, if you know what I mean.'

'Hullo, Eeyore,' said Pooh, coming up to them with his pole.

'Hullo, Pooh. Thank you for asking, but I shall be able to use it again in a day or two.'

'Use what?' said Pooh.

'What we are talking about.'

'I wasn't talking about anything,' said Pooh, looking puzzled.

'My mistake again. I thought you were saying how sorry you were about my tail, being all numb, and could you do anything to help?'

'No,' said Pooh. 'That wasn't me,' he said. He thought for a little and then suggested helpfully: 'Perhaps it was somebody else.'

'Well, thank him for me when you see him.'

Pooh looked anxiously at Christopher Robin.

'Pooh's found the North Pole,' said Christopher Robin. 'Isn't that lovely?'

Pooh looked modestly down.

'Is that it?' said Eeyore.

'Yes,' said Christopher Robin.

'Is that what we were looking for?'

'Yes,' said Pooh.

'Oh!' said Eeyore. 'Well, anyhow – it didn't rain,' he said.

They stuck the pole in the ground, and Christopher Robin tied a message on to it:

NORTH POLE
DICSOVERED BY
POOH
POOH FOUND IT

Then they all went home again. And I think, but I am not quite sure, that Roo had a hot bath and went straight to bed. But Pooh went back to his own house, and feeling very proud of what he had done, had a little something to revive himself.

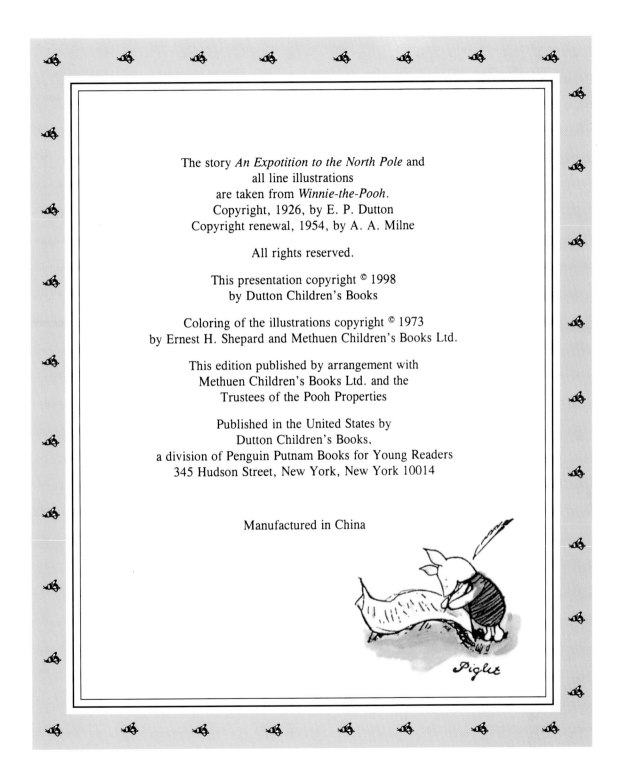

Pooh

A. A. MILNE

Pooh Goes Visiting and Pooh and Piglet Nearly Catch a Woozle

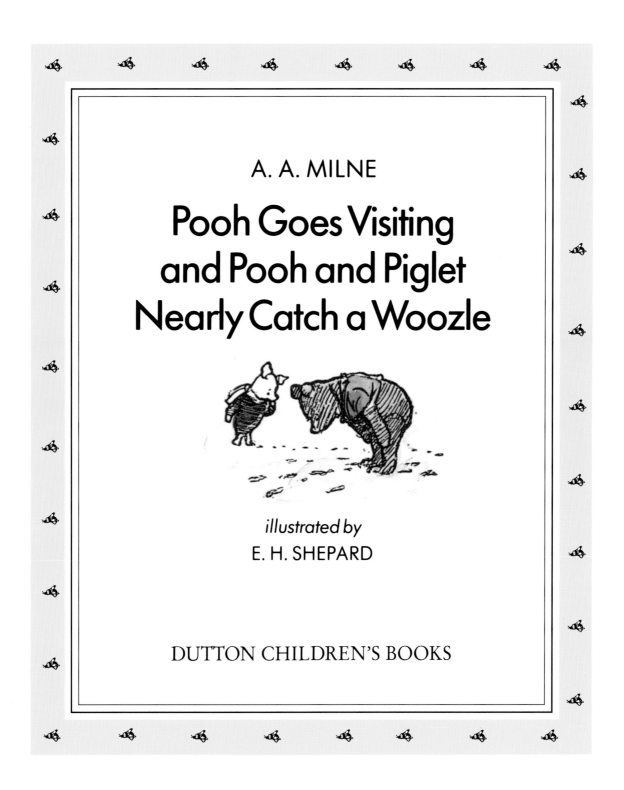

illustrated by

E. H. SHEPARD

DUTTON CHILDREN'S BOOKS

Pooh Goes Visiting and Pooh and Piglet Nearly Catch a Woozle

Edward Bear, known to his friends as Winnie-the-Pooh, or Pooh for short, was walking through the Forest one day, humming proudly to himself. He had made up a little hum that very morning, as he was doing his Stoutness Exercises in front of the glass: *Tra-la-la, tra-la-la*, as he stretched up as high as he could go, and then *Tra-la-la, tra-la – oh, help! – la*, as he tried to

reach his toes. After breakfast he had said it over and over to himself until he had learnt it off by heart, and now he was humming it right through, properly. It went like this:

Tra-la-la, tra-la-la,
Tra-la-la, tra-la-la,
Rum-tum-tiddle-um-um.
Tiddle-iddle, tiddle-iddle,
Tiddle-iddle, tiddle-iddle,
Rum-tum-tum-tiddle-um.

Well, he was humming this hum to himself, and walking gaily along, wondering what everybody else was doing, and what it felt like, being somebody else, when suddenly he came to a sandy bank, and in the bank was a large hole.

'Aha!' said Pooh. *(Rum-tum-tiddle-um-tum.)* 'If I know anything about anything, that hole means Rabbit,' he said, 'and Rabbit means Company,' he said, 'and Company means Food and Listening-to-Me-Humming and such like.

'Rum-tum-tum-tiddle-um.'

So he bent down, put his head into the hole, and called out: 'Is anybody at home?'

There was a sudden scuffling noise from inside the hole, and then silence.

'What I said was, "Is anybody at home?"' called out Pooh very loudly.

'No!' said a voice; and then added. 'You needn't shout so loud. I heard you quite well the first time.'

'Bother!' said Pooh. 'Isn't there anybody here at all?'

'Nobody.'

Winnie-the-Pooh took his head out of

the hole, and thought for a little, and he thought to himself, 'There must be somebody there, because somebody must have *said* "Nobody."' So he put his head back in the hole, and said: 'Hallo, Rabbit, isn't that you?'

'No,' said Rabbit, in a different sort of voice this time.

'But isn't that Rabbit's voice?'

'I don't *think* so,' said Rabbit. 'It isn't *meant* to be.'

'Oh!' said Pooh. He took his head out of the hole, and had another think, and then he put it back, and said: 'Well, could you very kindly tell me where Rabbit is?'

'He has gone to see his friend Pooh Bear, who is a great friend of his.'

'But this *is* Me!' said Bear, very much surprised.

'What sort of Me?'

'Pooh Bear.'

'Are you sure?' said Rabbit, still more surprised.

'Quite, quite sure,' said Pooh.

'Oh, well, then, come in.'

So Pooh pushed and pushed and pushed his

way through the hole, and at last he got in.

'You were quite right,' said Rabbit, looking at him all over. 'It *is* you. Glad to see you.'

'Who did you think it was?'

'Well, I wasn't sure. You know how it is in the Forest. One can't have *anybody* coming into one's house. One has to be *careful*. What about a mouthful of something?'

Pooh always liked a little something at eleven o'clock in the morning, and he was very glad to see Rabbit getting out the plates and mugs; and when Rabbit said, 'Honey or condensed milk with your bread?' he was so excited that he said, 'Both,' and then, so as not to seem greedy, he added, 'But don't bother about the bread, please.' And for a long time after that he said nothing . . . until at last, humming to himself in a rather sticky voice, he got up, shook Rabbit lovingly by the paw, and said that he must be going on.

'Must you?' said Rabbit politely.

'Well,' said Pooh, 'I could stay a little longer if it – if you—' and he tried very hard to look in the direction of the larder.

'As a matter of fact,' said Rabbit, 'I was going out myself directly.'

'Oh well, then, I'll be going on. Good-bye.'

'Well, good-bye, if you're sure you won't have any more.'

'*Is* there any more?' asked Pooh quickly.

Rabbit took the covers off the dishes, and said, 'No, there wasn't.'

'I thought not,' said Pooh, nodding to himself. 'Well, good-bye, I must be going on.'

So he started to climb out of the hole. He pulled with his front paws, and pushed with his back paws, and in a little while his nose was out in the open again . . . and then his ears . . . and then his front paws . . . and then his shoulders . . . and then—

'Oh, bother!' said Pooh. I shall have to go on.'
'Oh, help!' said Pooh. 'I'd better go back.'
'I can't do either!' said Pooh. 'Oh, help *and* bother!'

Now, by this time Rabbit wanted to go for a walk too, and finding the front door full, he went out by the back door, and came round to Pooh, and looked at him.

'Hallo, are you stuck?' he asked.

'N-no,' said Pooh carelessly. 'Just resting and thinking and humming to myself.'

'Here, give us a paw.'

Pooh Bear stretched out a paw, and Rabbit pulled and pulled and pulled. . . .

'*Ow!*' cried Pooh. 'You're hurting!'

'The fact is,' said Rabbit, 'you're stuck.'

'It all comes,' said Pooh crossly, 'of not having front doors big enough.'

'It all comes,' said Rabbit sternly, 'of eating too much. I thought at the time,' said Rabbit, 'only I didn't like to say anything,' said Rabbit, 'that one of us was eating too much,' said Rabbit, 'and I knew it wasn't *me*,' he said. 'Well, well, I shall go and fetch Christopher Robin.'

Christopher Robin lived at the other end of the Forest, and when he came back with

Rabbit, and saw the front half of Pooh, he said, 'Silly old Bear,' in such a loving voice that everybody felt quite hopeful again.

'I was just beginning to think,' said Bear, sniffing slightly, 'that Rabbit might never be able to use his front door again. And I should *hate* that,' he said.

'So should I,' said Rabbit.

'Use his front door again?' said Christopher Robin. 'Of course he'll use his front door again.'

'Good,' said Rabbit.

'If we can't pull you out, Pooh, we might push you back.'

Rabbit scratched his whiskers thoughtfully, and pointed out that, when once Pooh was pushed back, he was back, and of course nobody was more glad to see Pooh than *he* was, still there it was, some lived in trees and some lived underground, and—

'You mean I'd *never* get out?' said Pooh.

'I mean,' said Rabbit, 'that having got *so*

far, it seems a pity to waste it.'

Christopher Robin nodded.

'Then there's only one thing to be done,' he said. 'We shall have to wait for you to get thin again.'

'How long does getting thin take?' asked Pooh anxiously.

'About a week, I should think.'

'But I can't stay here for a *week*!'

'You can *stay* here all right, silly old Bear. It's getting you out which is so difficult.'

'We'll read to you,' said Rabbit cheerfully.

'And I hope it won't snow,' he added. 'And I say, old fellow, you're taking up a good deal of room in my house – *do* you mind if I use your back legs as a towel-horse? Because, I mean, there they are – doing nothing – and it would be very convenient just to hang the towels on them.'

'A week!' said Pooh gloomily. *'What about meals?'*

'I'm afraid no meals,' said Christopher Robin,

'because of getting thin quicker. But we *will* read to you.'

Bear began to sigh, and then found he couldn't because he was so tightly stuck; and a tear rolled down his eye, as he said:

'Then would you read a Sustaining Book, such as would help and comfort a Wedged Bear in Great Tightness?'

So for a week Christopher Robin read that sort of book at the North end of Pooh, and

Rabbit hung his washing on the South end . . .

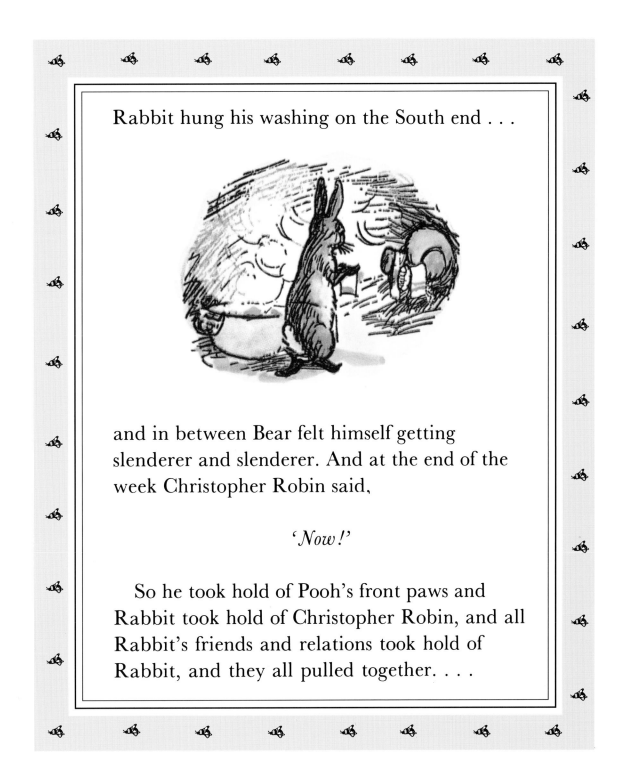

and in between Bear felt himself getting slenderer and slenderer. And at the end of the week Christopher Robin said,

'*Now!*'

So he took hold of Pooh's front paws and Rabbit took hold of Christopher Robin, and all Rabbit's friends and relations took hold of Rabbit, and they all pulled together. . . .

And for a long time Pooh
only said '*Ow!*' . . .
And '*Oh!*' . . .
And then, all of a sudden,
he said '*Pop!*' just as if a cork
were coming out of a bottle.
And Christopher Robin and
Rabbit and all Rabbit's friends
and relations went head-over-
heels backwards . . .

and on the top of them came
Winnie-the-Pooh – free!
   So, with a nod of thanks
to his friends,
he went on with his walk
through the forest,
humming proudly to himself.
But Christopher Robin
looked after him lovingly,
and said to himself,
'Silly old Bear!'

The Piglet lived in a very grand house in the middle of a beech-tree, and the beech-tree was in the middle of the Forest, and the Piglet

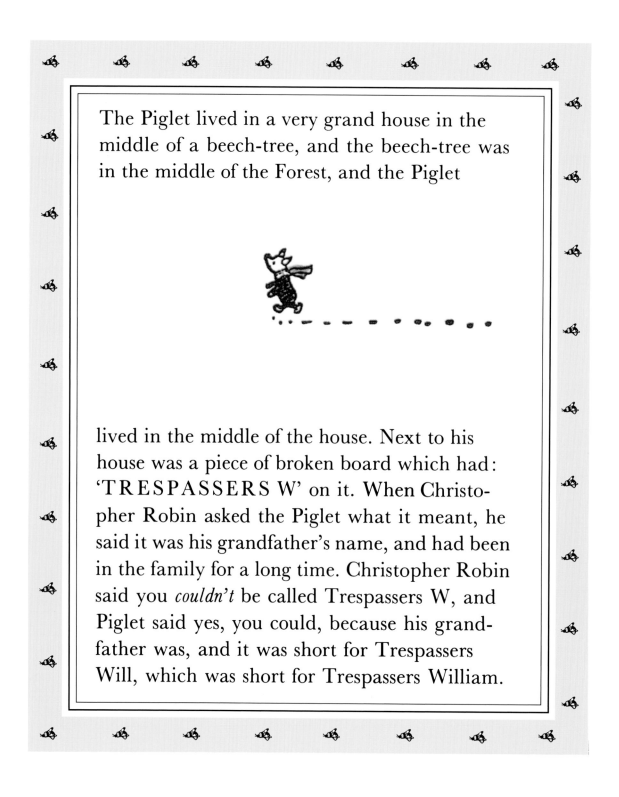

lived in the middle of the house. Next to his house was a piece of broken board which had: 'TRESPASSERS W' on it. When Christopher Robin asked the Piglet what it meant, he said it was his grandfather's name, and had been in the family for a long time. Christopher Robin said you *couldn't* be called Trespassers W, and Piglet said yes, you could, because his grandfather was, and it was short for Trespassers Will, which was short for Trespassers William.

237

And his grandfather had had two names in case he lost one – Trespassers after an uncle, and William after Trespassers.

'I've got two names,' said Christopher Robin carelessly.

'Well, there you are, that proves it,' said Piglet.

One fine winter's day when Piglet was brushing away the snow in front of his house, he happened to look up, and there was Winnie-the-Pooh. Pooh was walking round and round in a circle, thinking of something else, and when Piglet called to him, he just went on walking.

'Hallo!' said Piglet, 'what are *you* doing?'

'Hunting,' said Pooh.

'Hunting what?'

'Tracking something,' said Winnie-the-Pooh very mysteriously.

'Tracking what?' said Piglet, coming closer.

'That's just what I ask myself. I ask myself, What?'

'What do you think you'll answer?'

'I shall have to wait until I catch up with it,'

said Winnie-the-Pooh. 'Now, look there.' He pointed to the ground in front of him. 'What do you see there?'

'Tracks,' said Piglet. 'Paw-marks.' He gave a little squeak of excitement. 'Oh, Pooh! Do you think it's a – a – a Woozle?'

'It may be,' said Pooh. 'Sometimes it is, and sometimes it isn't. You can never tell with paw-marks.'

With these few words he went on tracking, and Piglet, after watching him for a minute or two, ran after him. Winnie-the-Pooh had come to a sudden stop, and was bending over the tracks in a puzzled sort of way.

'What's the matter?' asked Piglet.

'It's a very funny thing,' said Bear, 'but there seem to be *two* animals now. This – whatever-it-was – has been joined by another – whatever-it-is – and the two of them are now proceeding in company. Would you mind coming with me, Piglet, in case they turn out to be Hostile Animals?'

Piglet scratched his ear in a nice sort of way, and said that he had nothing to do until Friday, and would be delighted to come, in case it really *was* a Woozle.

'You mean, in case it really is two Woozles,' said Winnie-the-Pooh, and Piglet said that any-how he had nothing to do until Friday. So off they went together.

There was a small spinney of larch-trees just here, and it seemed as if the two Woozles, if that is what they were, had been going round this

241

spinney; so round this spinney went Pooh and Piglet after them; Piglet passing the time by telling Pooh what his Grandfather Trespassers W had done to Remove Stiffness after Tracking, and how his Grandfather Trespassers W had suffered in his later years from Shortness of Breath, and other matters of interest, and Pooh wondering what a Grandfather was like, and if perhaps this was Two Grandfathers they were after now, and, if so, whether  he would be allowed to take one home and keep it, and what Christopher Robin would say. And still the tracks went on in front of them. . . .

Suddenly Winnie-the-Pooh stopped, and pointed excitedly in front of him. '*Look!*'

'*What?*' said Piglet, with a jump. And then,

to show that he hadn't been frightened, he jumped up and down once or twice more in an exercising sort of way.

'The tracks!' said Pooh. *'A third animal has joined the other two!'*

'Pooh!' cried Piglet. 'Do you think it is another Woozle?'

'No,' said Pooh, 'because it makes different marks. It is either Two Woozles and one, as it might be, Wizzle, or Two, as it might be, Wizzles and one, if so it is, Woozle. Let us continue to follow them.'

So they went on, feeling just a little anxious now, in case the three animals in front of them were of Hostile Intent. And Piglet wished very much that his Grandfather T. W. were there, instead of elsewhere, and Pooh thought how nice it would be if they met Christopher Robin suddenly but quite accidentally, and only because he liked Christopher Robin so much. And then, all of a sudden, Winnie-the-Pooh stopped again, and licked the tip of his nose in a cooling manner, for he was feeling more hot and anxious than ever in his life before. *There were four animals in front of them!*

'Do you see, Piglet? Look at their tracks! Three, as it were, Woozles, and one, as it was, Wizzle. *Another Woozle has joined them!*'

And so it seemed to be. There were the tracks; crossing over each other here, getting muddled up with each other there; but, quite plainly every now and then, the tracks of four sets of paws.

'I *think*,' said Piglet, when he had licked the tip of his nose too, and found that it brought very little comfort, 'I *think* that I have just remembered something. I have just remembered something that I forgot to do yesterday and shan't be able to do to-morrow. So I suppose I really ought to go back and do it now.'

'We'll do it this afternoon, and I'll come with you,' said Pooh.

'It isn't the sort of thing you can do in the afternoon,' said Piglet quickly. 'It's a very particular morning thing, that has to be done in the morning, and, if possible, between the hours of— What would you say the time was?'

'About twelve,' said Winnie-the-Pooh, looking at the sun.

'Between, as I was saying, the hours of twelve and twelve five. So, really, dear old Pooh, if you'll excuse me— *What's that?*'

Pooh looked up at the sky, and then, as he heard the whistle again, he looked up into the branches of a big oak-tree, and then he saw a friend of his.

'It's Christopher Robin,' he said.

'Ah, then you'll be all right,' said Piglet. 'You'll be quite safe with *him*. Good-bye,' and he trotted off home as quickly as he could, very glad to be Out of All Danger again.

Christopher Robin came slowly down his tree.

'Silly old Bear,' he said, 'what *were* you doing? First you went round the spinney twice by yourself, and then Piglet ran after you and you went round again together, and then you were just going round a fourth time—'

'Wait a moment,' said Winnie-the-Pooh, holding up his paw.

He sat down and thought, in the most thoughtful way he could think. Then he fitted his paw into one of the Tracks . . . and then he scratched his nose twice, and stood up.

'Yes,' said Winnie-the-Pooh.

'I see now,' said Winnie-the-Pooh.

'I have been Foolish and Deluded,' said he, 'and I am a Bear of No Brain at All.'

'You're the Best Bear in All the World,' said Christopher Robin soothingly.

'Am I?' said Pooh hopefully. And then he brightened up suddenly. 'Anyhow,' he said, 'it is nearly Luncheon Time.'

So he went home for it.

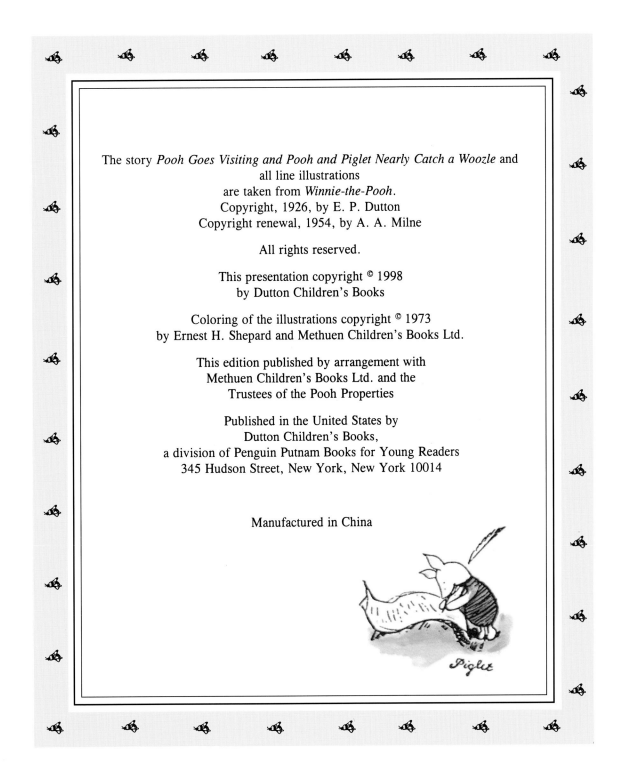

Pooh

A. A. MILNE

Christopher Robin Gives Pooh a Party

illustrated by

E. H. SHEPARD

DUTTON CHILDREN'S BOOKS

Christopher Robin
Gives Pooh a Party

It had rained and rained so that
the tree that was Piglet's home
was entirely surrounded by water.
He was rescued by Pooh, who set
out first on a honey jar (which
he named The Floating Bear*) and*
then in Christopher Robin's
umbrella (which he named
The Brain of Pooh*).*

One day when the sun had come back
over the Forest, bringing with it the scent
of may, and all the streams of the
Forest were tinkling happily to find
themselves their own pretty shape again,

and the little pools lay dreaming of the life they had seen and the big things they had done, and in the warmth and quiet of the Forest the cuckoo was trying over his voice carefully and listening to see if he liked it, and wood-pigeons were complaining gently to themselves in their lazy comfortable way that it was the other fellow's fault, but it didn't matter very much; on such a day as this Christopher Robin whistled in a special way he had, and Owl came flying out of the Hundred Acre Wood to see what was wanted.

'Owl,' said Christopher Robin, 'I am going to give a party.'

'You are, are you?' said Owl.

'And it's to be a special sort of party, because it's because of what Pooh did when he did what he did to save Piglet from the flood.'

'Oh, that's what it's for, is it?' said Owl.

'Yes, so will you tell Pooh as quickly

as you can, and all the others, because it
will be to-morrow?'

'Oh, it will, will it?' said Owl, still
being as helpful as possible.

'So will you go and tell them, Owl?'

Owl tried to think of something very
wise to say, but couldn't, so he flew off
to tell the others. And the first person
he told was Pooh.

'Pooh,' he said, 'Christopher Robin
is giving a party.'

'Oh!' said Pooh. And then seeing that Owl
expected him to say something else,
he said, 'Will there be those little cake things
with pink sugar icing?'

Owl felt that it was rather beneath him
to talk about little cake things
with pink sugar icing, so he told Pooh
exactly what Christopher Robin had said,
and flew off to Eeyore.

'A party for me?' thought Pooh to himself.
'How grand!' And he began

to wonder if all the other animals
would know that it was a special
Pooh party, and if Christopher Robin
had told them about *The Floating
Bear* and the *Brain of Pooh* and all

the wonderful ships he had invented
and sailed on, and he began to think
how awful it would be if everybody
had forgotten about it, and nobody
quite knew what the party was for;
and the more he thought like this,

the more the party got muddled in his mind, like a dream when nothing goes right. And the dream began to sing itself over in his head until it became a sort of song. It was an

ANXIOUS POOH SONG

3 Cheers for Pooh!
(For Who?)
For Pooh –
(Why what did he do?)
I thought you knew;
He saved his friend from a wetting!
3 Cheers for Bear!
(For where?)
For Bear –
He couldn't swim,
But he rescued him!
(He rescued who?)
Oh, listen, do!
I am talking of Pooh –
(Of who?)
Of Pooh!
(I'm sorry I keep forgetting.)

Well, Pooh was a Bear of Enormous Brain –
(Just say it again!)
Of enormous brain –
(Of enormous what?)
Well, he ate a lot,
And I don't know if he could swim or not,
But he managed to float
On a sort of boat
(On a sort of what?)
Well, a sort of pot –
So now let's give him three hearty cheers
(So now let's give him three hearty whiches!)
And hope he'll be with us for years and years,

And grow in health and wisdom and riches!
3 Cheers for Pooh!
(For who?)
For Pooh –
3 Cheers for Bear!
(For where?)
For Bear –

3 Cheers for the wonderful Winnie-the-Pooh!
(*Just tell me, somebody* – WHAT DID HE DO?)

While this was going on inside him,
Owl was talking to Eeyore.

'Eeyore,' said Owl, 'Christopher Robin
is giving a party.'

'Very interesting,' said Eeyore.

'I suppose they will be sending me down
the odd bits which got trodden on. Kind and
thoughtful. Not at all, don't mention it.'

'There is an Invitation for you.'

'What's that like?'

'An Invitation!'

'Yes, I heard you. Who dropped it?'

'This isn't anything to eat, it's asking you to the party. To-morrow.'

Eeyore shook his head slowly.

'You mean Piglet. The little fellow with the excited ears. That's Piglet. I'll tell him.'

'No, no!' said Owl, getting quite fussy. 'It's you!'

'Are you sure?'

'Of course I'm sure. Christopher

Robin said "All of them! Tell all of them".'
   'All of them, except Eeyore?'
   'All of them,' said Owl sulkily.
   'Ah!' said Eeyore. 'A mistake, no
doubt, but still, I shall come. Only
don't blame *me* if it rains.'

But it didn't rain. Christopher Robin
had made a long table out of some long
pieces of wood, and they all sat round it.

Christopher Robin sat at one end, and
Pooh sat at the other, and between them
on one side were Owl and Eeyore and Piglet,

and between them on the other side were
Rabbit, and Roo and Kanga. And all Rabbit's
friends and relations spread themselves
about on the grass, and waited hopefully
in case anybody spoke to them, or
dropped anything, or asked them the time.

   It was the first party to which Roo had
ever been, and he was very excited. As soon

as ever they had sat down he began to talk.

'Hallo, Pooh!' he squeaked.

'Hallo, Roo!' said Pooh.

Roo jumped up and down in his seat for a little while and then began again.

'Hallo, Piglet!' he squeaked.

Piglet waved a paw at him, being too busy to say anything.

'Hallo, Eeyore!' said Roo.

Eeyore nodded gloomily at him. 'It will rain soon, you see if it doesn't,' he said.

Roo looked to see if it didn't, and it didn't, so he said 'Hallo, Owl!' and Owl said 'Hallo, my little fellow,' in a kindly way, and went on telling Christopher Robin about an accident which had nearly happened to a friend of his whom Christopher Robin didn't know, and Kanga said to Roo, 'Drink up your milk first, dear, and talk afterwards.' So Roo, who was drinking his milk, tried to say that he could do both at once . . . and had to be patted on the back and dried for quite a long time afterwards.

When they had all nearly eaten enough, Christopher Robin banged on the table with his spoon, and everybody stopped talking and was very silent, except Roo who was just finishing a loud attack of hiccups and trying to look as if it was one of Rabbit's relations.

'This party,' said Christopher Robin, 'is a party because of what someone did, and we all know who it was, and it's his party, because of what he did, and I've got a present for him and here it is.' Then he felt about a little and whispered, 'Where is it?'

While he was looking Eeyore coughed in an impressive way and began to speak.

'Friends,' he said, 'including oddments, it is a great pleasure, or perhaps I had better say it has been a pleasure so far, to see you at my party. What I did was nothing. Any of you – except Rabbit and Owl and Kanga – would have done the same. Oh, and Pooh. My remarks do not,

of course, apply to Piglet and Roo, because they are too small. Any of you would have done the same. But it just happened to be Me. It was not, I need hardly say, with an idea of getting what Christopher Robin is looking for now' – and he put his front leg to his mouth and said in a loud whisper, 'Try under the table' – 'that I did what I did – but because I feel that we should all do what we can to help. I feel that we should all—'

'H – hup!' said Roo accidentally.

'Roo, dear!' said Kanga reproachfully.

'Was it me?' asked Roo, a little surprised.

'What's Eeyore talking about?' Piglet whispered to Pooh.

'I don't know,' said Pooh rather dolefully.

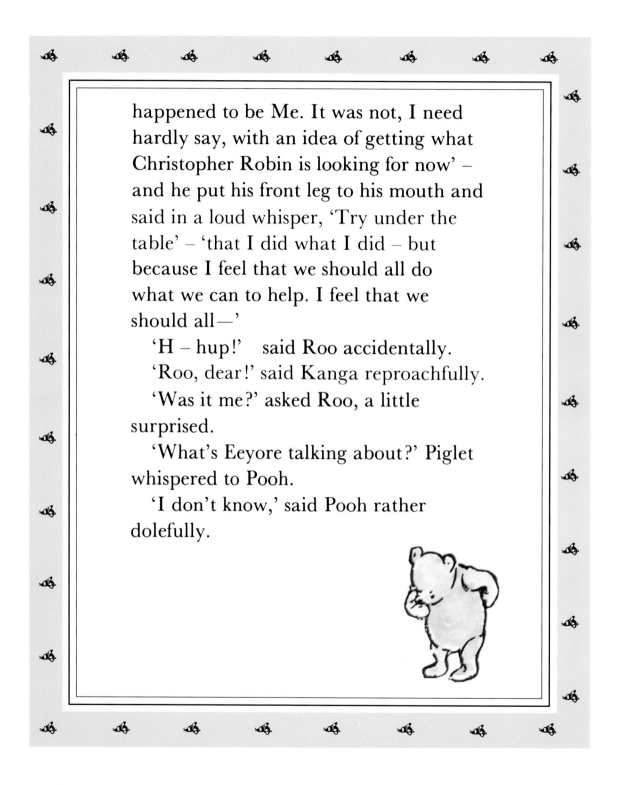

'I thought this was *your* party.'

'I thought it was *once*. But I suppose
it isn't.'

'I'd sooner it was yours than Eeyore's,'
said Piglet.

'So would I,' said Pooh.

'H – hup!' said Roo again.

'AS – I – WAS – SAYING,' said Eeyore
loudly and sternly, 'as I was saying when
I was interrupted by various Loud Sounds,
I feel that—'

'Here it is!' cried Christopher Robin excitedly. 'Pass it down to silly old Pooh. It's for Pooh.'

'For Pooh?' said Eeyore.

'Of course it is. The best bear in all the world.'

'I might have known,' said Eeyore. 'After all, one can't complain. I have my friends. Somebody spoke to me only yesterday. And was it last week or the week before that Rabbit bumped into me and said "Bother!" The Social Round. Always something going on.'

Nobody was listening, for they were all saying, 'Open it, Pooh.' 'What is it, Pooh?' 'I know what it is,' 'No, you don't,' and other helpful remarks of this sort. And of course Pooh was opening it as quickly as ever he could, but without cutting the string, because you never know when a bit of string might be Useful. At last it was undone.

When Pooh saw what it was, he nearly fell down, he was so pleased. It was a

Special Pencil Case. There were pencils in it marked 'B' for Bear, and pencils marked 'HB' for Helping Bear, and pencils marked

'BB' for Brave Bear. There was a knife for sharpening the pencils, an india-rubber for rubbing out anything which you

had spelt wrong, and a ruler for ruling lines for the words to walk on, and inches marked on the ruler in case you wanted to know how many inches anything was, and Blue Pencils and Red Pencils and Green Pencils for saying special things in blue and red and green. And all these lovely things were in little pockets of their own in a Special Case which shut with a click when you clicked it. And they were all for Pooh.

'Oh!' said Pooh.

'Oh, Pooh!' said everybody else except Eeyore.

'Thank you,' growled Pooh.

But Eeyore was saying to himself, 'This writing business. Pencils and what-not. Over-rated, if you ask me. Silly stuff. Nothing in it.'

Pooh

Later on, when they had all said 'Good-bye' and 'Thank-you' to Christopher Robin,

Pooh and Piglet walked home thoughtfully together in the golden evening, and for a long time they were silent.

'When you wake up in the morning, Pooh,' said Piglet at last, 'what's the first thing you say to yourself?'

'What's for breakfast?' said Pooh. 'What do *you* say, Piglet?'

'I say, I wonder what's going to happen exciting *today*?' said Piglet.

Pooh nodded thoughtfully.

'It's the same thing,' he said.

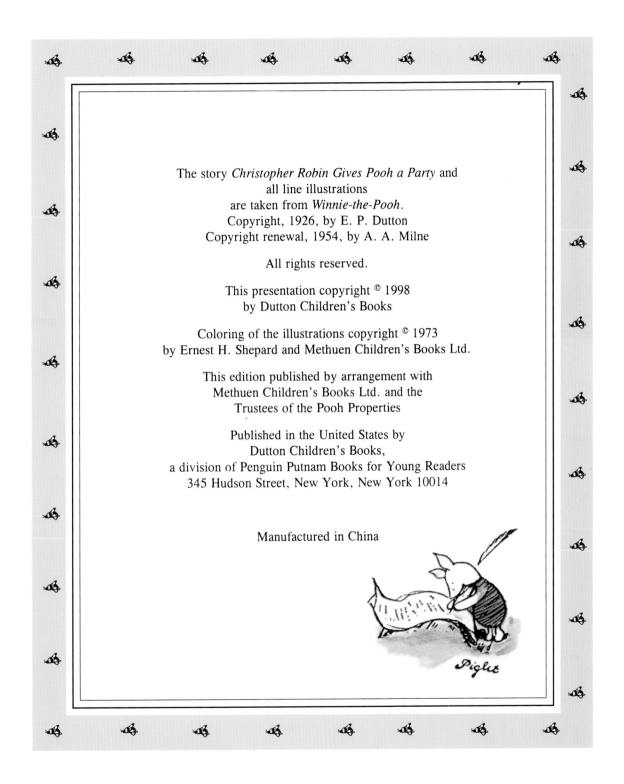

Pooh

A. A. MILNE

Pooh Invents
a New Game

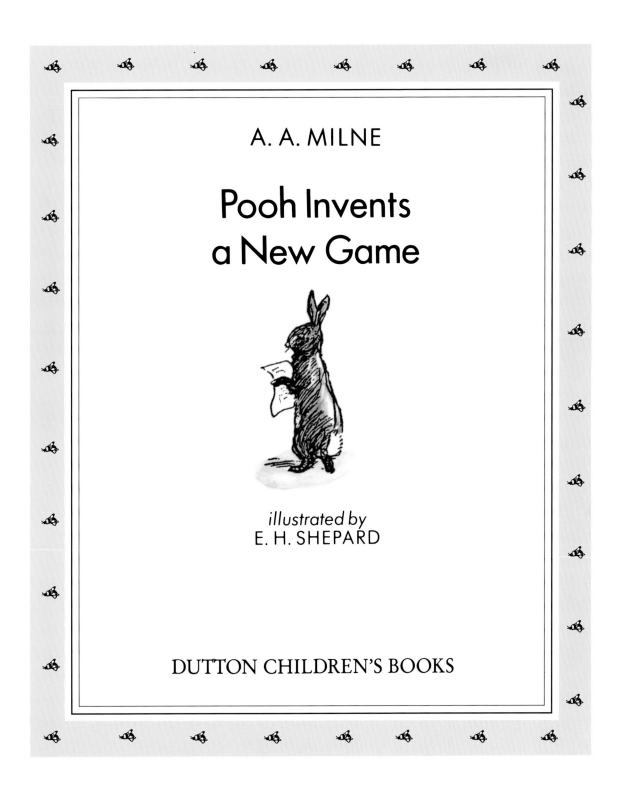

illustrated by
E. H. SHEPARD

DUTTON CHILDREN'S BOOKS

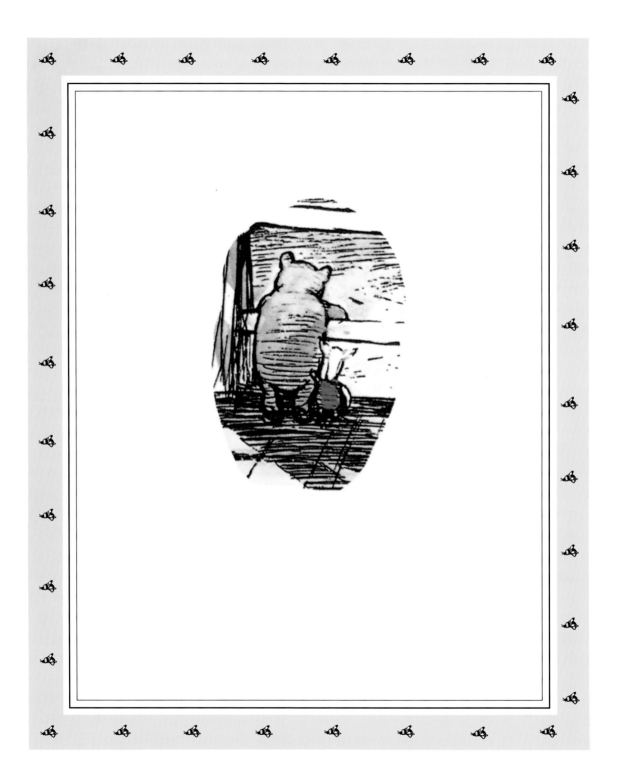

Pooh Invents a New Game

By the time it came to the edge of the Forest
the stream had grown up, so that it was
almost a river, and, being grown-up, it did
not run and jump and sparkle along as it used
to do when it was younger, but moved more
slowly. For it knew now where it was going,
and it said to itself, 'There is no hurry.
We shall get there some day.' But all the
little streams higher up in the Forest went
this way and that, quickly, eagerly, having
so much to find out before it was too late.

There was a broad track, almost as broad as a road, leading from the Outland to the Forest, but before it could come to the Forest, it had to cross this river. So, where it crossed, there was a wooden bridge, almost as broad as a road, with wooden rails on each side of it. Christopher Robin could just get his chin on to the top rail, if he wanted to, but it was more fun to stand on the bottom rail, so that he could lean right over, and watch the river slipping slowly away beneath him. Pooh could get his chin on to the bottom rail if he wanted to, but it was more fun to lie down and get his head under it, and watch the river slipping slowly away beneath him. And this was the only way in which Piglet and Roo could watch the river at all, because they were too small to reach the bottom rail. So they would lie down and watch it . . . and it slipped away very slowly, being in no hurry to get there.

One day, when Pooh was walking towards this

bridge, he was trying to make up a piece of
poetry about fir-cones, because there they were,
lying about on each side of him, and he felt
singy. So he picked a fir-cone up, and looked
at it, and said to himself, 'This is a very
good fir-cone, and something ought to rhyme to
it.' But he couldn't think of anything. And then
this came into his head suddenly:

> Here is a myst'ry
> About a little fir-tree.
> Owl says it's *his* tree,
> And Kanga says it's *her* tree.

'Which doesn't make sense,' said Pooh,
'because Kanga doesn't live in a tree.'

He had just come to the bridge; and not
looking where he was going, he tripped over
something, and the fir-cone jerked out of
his paw into the river.

'Bother,' said Pooh, as it floated slowly
under the bridge, and he went back to get
another fir-cone which had a rhyme to it.

But then he thought that he would just look
at the river instead, because it was a
peaceful sort of day, so he lay down and
looked at it, and it slipped slowly away
beneath him . . . and suddenly, there was his
fir-cone slipping away too.

   'That's funny,' said Pooh. 'I dropped it
on the other side,' said Pooh, 'and it came out
on this side! I wonder if it would do it
again?' And he went back for some more fir-
cones.

   It did. It kept on doing it. Then he
dropped two in at once, and leant over the

bridge to see which of them would come out
first; and one of them did; but as they were
both the same size, he didn't know if it was
the one which he wanted to win, or the other
one. So the next time he dropped one big one
and one little one, and the big one came out
first, which was what he had said it would do,
and the little one came out last, which was
what he had said it would do, so he had won
twice . . . and when he went home for tea, he had
won thirty-six and lost twenty-eight, which
meant that he was—that he had—well, you take
twenty-eight from thirty-six, and *that's* what
he was. Instead of the other way round.

And that was the beginning of the game
called Poohsticks, which Pooh invented, and
which he and his friends used to play on the
edge of the Forest. But they played with
sticks instead of fir-cones, because they were
easier to mark.

Now one day Pooh and Piglet and Rabbit and
Roo were all playing Poohsticks together. They

had dropped their sticks in when Rabbit said 'Go!' and then they had hurried across to the other side of the bridge, and now they were all leaning over the edge, waiting to see whose stick would come out first. But it was a long time coming, because the river was very lazy that day, and hardly seemed to mind if it didn't ever get there at all.

'I can see mine!' cried Roo. 'No, I can't. It's something else. Can you see yours, Piglet? I thought I could see mine, but I couldn't. There it is! No, it isn't. Can you see yours, Pooh?'

'No,' said Pooh.

'I expect my stick's stuck,' said Roo. 'Rabbit, my stick's stuck. Is your stick stuck, Piglet?'

'They always take longer than you think,' said Rabbit.

'How long do you *think* they'll take?' asked Roo.

'I can see yours, Piglet,' said Pooh suddenly.

'Mine's a sort of greyish one,' said Piglet, not daring to lean too far over in case he fell in.

'Yes, that's what I can see. It's coming over on to my side.'

Rabbit leant over further than ever, looking for his and Roo wriggled up and down, calling out 'Come on, stick! Stick, stick, stick!' and Piglet got very excited because his was the only one which had been seen, and that meant that he was winning.

'It's coming!' said Pooh.

'Are you *sure* it's mine?' squeaked Piglet excitedly.

'Yes, because it's grey. A big grey one. Here it comes! A very—big—grey—Oh, no, it isn't, it's Eeyore.'

And out floated Eeyore.

'Eeyore!' cried everybody.

Looking very calm, very dignified, with his legs in the air, came Eeyore from beneath the bridge.

'It's Eeyore!' cried Roo, terribly excited.

'Is that so?' said Eeyore, getting caught up by a little eddy, and turning slowly round three times. 'I wondered.'

'I didn't know you were playing,' said Roo.

'I'm not,' said Eeyore.

'Eeyore, what *are* you doing there?' said Rabbit.

'I'll give you three guesses, Rabbit. Digging holes in the ground? Wrong. Leaping from branch to branch of a young oak-tree? Wrong. Waiting for somebody to help me out of the river? Right. Give Rabbit time, and he'll always get the answer.'

'But, Eeyore,' said Pooh in distress, 'what can we—I mean, how shall we—do you think if we—'

'Yes,' said Eeyore. 'One of those would be just the thing. Thank you, Pooh.'

'He's going *round* and *round*,' said Roo, much impressed.

'And why not?' said Eeyore coldly.

'I can swim too,' said Roo proudly.

'Not round and round,' said Eeyore. 'It's much more difficult. I didn't want to come swimming at all to-day,' he went on, revolving slowly. 'But if, when in, I decide to practise a slight circular movement from right to left— or perhaps I should say,' he added, as he got into another eddy, 'from left to right, just as it happens to occur to me, it is nobody's business but my own.'

There was a moment's silence while everybody thought.

'I've got a sort of idea,' said Pooh at last, 'but I don't suppose it's a very good one.'

'I don't suppose it is either,' said Eeyore.

'Go on, Pooh,' said Rabbit. 'Let's have it.'

'Well, if we all threw stones and things into the river on *one* side of Eeyore, the stones would make waves, and the waves would wash him to the other side.'

'That's a very good idea,' said Rabbit, and Pooh looked happy again.

'Very,' said Eeyore. 'When I want to be washed, Pooh, I'll let you know.'

'Supposing we hit him by mistake?' said Piglet anxiously.

'Or supposing you missed him by mistake,' said Eeyore. 'Think of all the possibilities, Piglet, before you settle down to enjoy yourselves.'

But Pooh had got the biggest stone he could carry, and was leaning over the bridge, holding it in his paws.

'I'm not throwing it, I'm dropping it, Eeyore,' he explained. 'And then I can't miss—I mean I can't hit you. *Could* you stop turning round for a moment, because it muddles me rather?'

'No,' said Eeyore. 'I *like* turning round.'

Rabbit began to feel that it was time he took command.

'Now, Pooh,' he said, 'when I say "Now!" you can drop it. Eeyore, when I say "Now!" Pooh will drop his stone.'

'Thank you very much, Rabbit, but I expect I shall know.'

'Are you ready, Pooh? Piglet, give Pooh a little more room. Get back a bit there, Roo. Are you ready?'

'No,' said Eeyore.

'*Now!*' said Rabbit.

Pooh dropped his stone. There was a loud splash, and Eeyore disappeared . . .

It was an anxious moment for the watchers on the bridge. They looked and looked . . . and even the sight of Piglet's stick coming out a little in front of Rabbit's didn't cheer them up as much as you would have expected. And then, just as Pooh was beginning to think that he must have chosen the wrong stone or the wrong river or the wrong day for his Idea, something grey showed for a moment by the river bank . . . and it got slowly bigger and bigger . . . and at last it was Eeyore coming out.

With a shout they rushed off the bridge, and pushed and pulled at him; and soon he was standing among them again on dry land.

'Oh, Eeyore, you *are* wet!' said Piglet, feeling him.

Eeyore shook himself, and asked somebody to explain to Piglet what happened when you had been inside a river for quite a long time.

'Well done, Pooh,' said Rabbit kindly. 'That was a good idea of yours.'

'What was?' asked Eeyore.

'Hooshing you to the bank like that.'

'*Hooshing* me?' said Eeyore in surprise. 'Hooshing *me*? You didn't think I was *hooshed*, did you? I dived. Pooh dropped a large stone on me, and so as not to be struck heavily on the chest, I dived and swam to the bank.'

'You didn't really,' whispered Piglet to Pooh, so as to comfort him.

'I didn't *think* I did,' said Pooh anxiously.

'It's just Eeyore,' said Piglet. '*I* thought your Idea was a very good Idea.'

Pooh began to feel a little more comfortable, because when you are a Bear of Very Little Brain, and you Think of Things, you find sometimes that a Thing which seemed very Thingish inside you is quite different when it gets out into the open and has other people looking at it. And, anyhow, Eeyore *was* in the river, and now he *wasn't*, so he hadn't done any harm.

'How did you fall in, Eeyore?' asked Rabbit, as he dried him with Piglet's handkerchief.

'I didn't,' said Eeyore.

'I was BOUNCED,' said Eeyore.

'Oh,' said Roo excitedly, 'did somebody push you?'

'Somebody BOUNCED me. I was just thinking by the side of the river—thinking, if any of you know what that means—when I received a loud BOUNCE.'

'Oh, Eeyore!' said everybody.

'Are you sure you didn't slip?' asked
Rabbit wisely.

'Of course I slipped. If you're standing
on the slippery bank of a river, and somebody
BOUNCES you loudly from behind, you slip.
What did you think I did?'

'But who did it?' asked Roo.

Eeyore didn't answer.

'I expect it was Tigger,' said Piglet
nervously.

'But, Eeyore,' said Pooh, 'was it a Joke,
or an Accident? I mean—'

'I didn't stop to ask, Pooh. Even at the very bottom of the river I didn't stop to say to myself, "*Is* this a Hearty Joke, or is it the Merest Accident?" I just floated to the surface, and said to myself, "It's wet." If you know what I mean.'

'And where was Tigger?' asked Rabbit.

Before Eeyore could answer, there was a loud noise behind them, and through the hedge came Tigger himself.

'Hallo, everybody,' said Tigger cheerfully.

'Hallo, Tigger,' said Roo.

Rabbit became very important suddenly.

'Tigger,' he said solemnly, 'what happened just now?'

'Just when?' said Tigger a little uncomfortably.

'When you bounced Eeyore into the river.'

'I didn't bounce him.'

'You bounced me,' said Eeyore gruffly.

'I didn't really. I had a cough, and I happened to be behind Eeyore, and I said "*Grrrr—oppp—ptschschschz*".'

'Why?' said Rabbit, helping Piglet up, and dusting him. 'It's all right, Piglet.'

'It took me by surprise,' said Piglet nervously.

'That's what I call bouncing,' said Eeyore. 'Taking people by surprise. Very unpleasant habit. I don't mind Tigger being in the Forest,' he went on, 'because it's a large Forest, and there's plenty of room to bounce in it. But I don't see why he should come into *my* little corner of it, and bounce there. It isn't as if there was anything very wonderful about my little corner. Of course for people who like cold, wet, ugly bits it *is* something rather

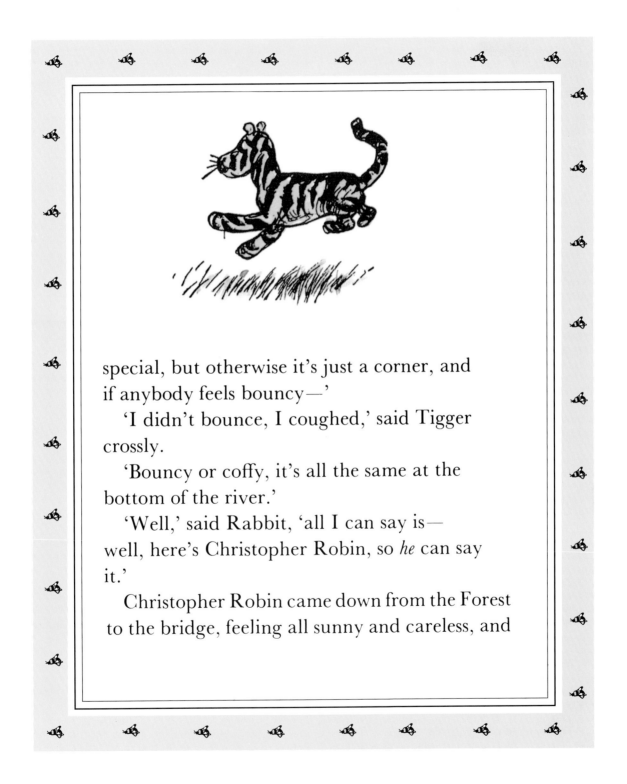

special, but otherwise it's just a corner, and if anybody feels bouncy—'

'I didn't bounce, I coughed,' said Tigger crossly.

'Bouncy or coffy, it's all the same at the bottom of the river.'

'Well,' said Rabbit, 'all I can say is—well, here's Christopher Robin, so *he* can say it.'

Christopher Robin came down from the Forest to the bridge, feeling all sunny and careless, and just as if twice nineteen didn't matter a bit, as it didn't on such a happy afternoon, and he thought that if he stood on the bottom rail of the bridge, and leant over, and watched the river slipping slowly away beneath him, then he would suddenly know everything that there was to be known, and he would be able to tell Pooh, who wasn't quite sure about some of it. But when he got to the bridge and saw all the animals there, then he knew that it wasn't that kind of afternoon, but the other kind, when you wanted to *do* something.

'It's like this, Christopher Robin,' began Rabbit. 'Tigger—'

'No, I didn't,' said Tigger.

'Well, anyhow, there I was,' said Eeyore.

'But I don't think he meant to,' said Pooh.

'He just *is* bouncy,' said Piglet, 'and he can't help it.'

'Try bouncing *me*, Tigger,' said Roo eagerly. 'Eeyore, Tigger's going to try *me*. Piglet, do you think—'

'Yes, yes,' said Rabbit, 'we don't all want to speak at once. The point is, what does Christopher Robin think about it?'

'All I did was I coughed,' said Tigger.

'He bounced,' said Eeyore.

'Well, I sort of boffed,' said Tigger.

'Hush!' said Rabbit, holding up his paw. 'What does Christopher Robin think about it all? That's the point.'

'Well,' said Christopher Robin, not quite sure what it was all about. '*I* think—'

'Yes?' said everybody.

'*I* think we all ought to play Poohsticks.'

So they did. And Eeyore, who had never played it before, won more times than anybody else; and Roo fell in twice, the first time by accident and the second time on purpose, because he suddenly saw Kanga coming from the Forest, and he knew he'd have to go to bed anyhow. So then Rabbit said he'd go with them; and Tigger and Eeyore went off together, because Eeyore wanted to tell Tigger How to

Win at Poohsticks, which you do by letting your stick drop in a twitchy sort of way, if you understand what I mean, Tigger; and Christopher Robin and Pooh and Piglet were left on the bridge by themselves.

For a long time they looked at the river beneath them, saying nothing, and the river said nothing too, for it felt very quiet and peaceful on this summer afternoon.

'Tigger is all right, *really*,' said Piglet lazily.

'Of course he is,' said Christopher Robin.

'Everybody is *really*,' said Pooh. 'That's what *I* think,' said Pooh. 'But I don't suppose I'm right,' he said.

'Of course you are,' said Christopher Robin.

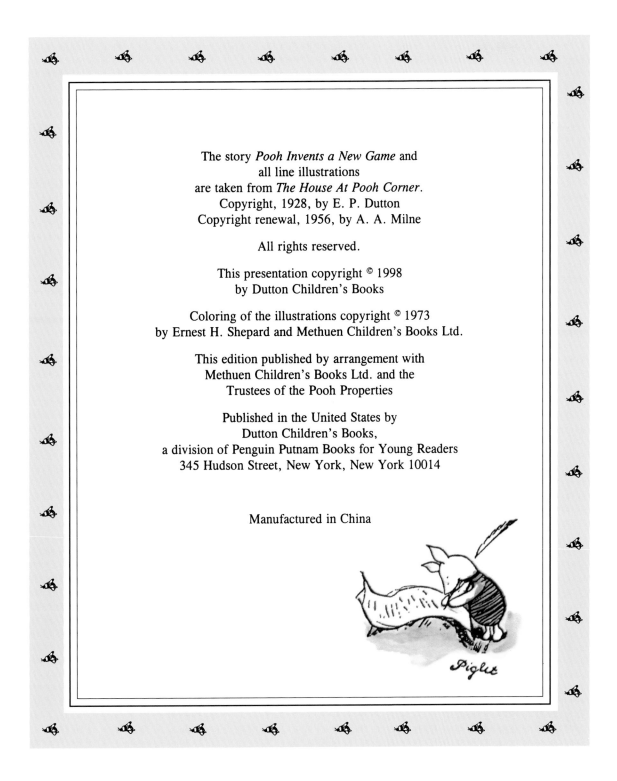

Pool

A. A. MILNE

Kanga and Baby Roo
Come
to the Forest

illustrated by

E. H. SHEPARD

DUTTON CHILDREN'S BOOKS

Kanga and Baby Roo
Come to the Forest

Nobody seemed to know where they came from, but there they were in the Forest: Kanga and Baby Roo. When Pooh asked Christopher Robin, 'How did they come here?'

Christopher Robin said,
'In the Usual Way, if
you know what I mean,
Pooh,' and Pooh, who
didn't, said 'Oh!' Then
he nodded his head
twice and said, 'In
the Usual Way. Ah!'

Then he went to call
upon his friend Piglet
to see what *he*
thought about
it. And at Piglet's
house he found Rabbit. So they all talked about
it together.

'What I don't like about it is this,' said
Rabbit. 'Here are we – you, Pooh, and you,
Piglet, and Me – and suddenly—'

'And Eeyore,' said Pooh.

'And Eeyore – and then suddenly—'

'And Owl,' said Pooh.

'And Owl – and then all of a sudden—'

'Oh, and Eeyore,' said Pooh. 'I was forgetting *him*.'

'Here – we – are,' said Rabbit very slowly and carefully, 'all – of – us, and then, suddenly, we wake up one morning, and what do we find? We find a Strange Animal among us. An animal of whom we had never even heard before! An animal who carries her family about with her in her pocket! Suppose *I* carried *my* family about with me in *my* pocket, how many pockets should I want?'

'Sixteen,' said Piglet.

'Seventeen, isn't it?' said Rabbit. 'And one more for a handkerchief – that's eighteen. Eighteen pockets in one suit! I haven't time.'

There was a long and thoughtful silence . . . and then Pooh, who had been frowning very hard for some minutes, said: '*I* make it fifteen.'

'What?' said Rabbit.

'Fifteen.'

'Fifteen what?'

'Your family.'

'What about them?'

Pooh rubbed his nose and said that he thought Rabbit had been talking about his family.

'Did I?' said Rabbit carelessly.

'Yes, you said—'

'Never mind, Pooh,' said Piglet impatiently. 'The question is, What are we to do about Kanga?'

'Oh, I see,' said Pooh.

'The best way,' said Rabbit, 'would be this. The best way would be to steal Baby Roo and hide him, and then when Kanga says, "Where's Baby Roo?" we say, "*Aha!*"'

'*Aha!*' said Pooh, practising. '*Aha! Aha!* . . . Of course,' he went on, 'we could say "Aha!" even if we hadn't stolen Baby Roo.'

'Pooh,' said Rabbit kindly, 'you haven't any brain.

'I know,' said Pooh humbly.

'We say "*Aha!*" so that Kanga knows that *we* know where Baby Roo is. "*Aha!*" means

"We'll tell you where Baby Roo is, if you promise to go away from the Forest and never come back." Now don't talk while I think.'

Pooh went into a corner and tried saying 'Aha!' in that sort of voice. Sometimes it seemed to him that it did mean what Rabbit said, and sometimes it seemed to him that it didn't. 'I suppose it's just practice,' he thought. 'I wonder if Kanga will have to practise too so as to understand it.'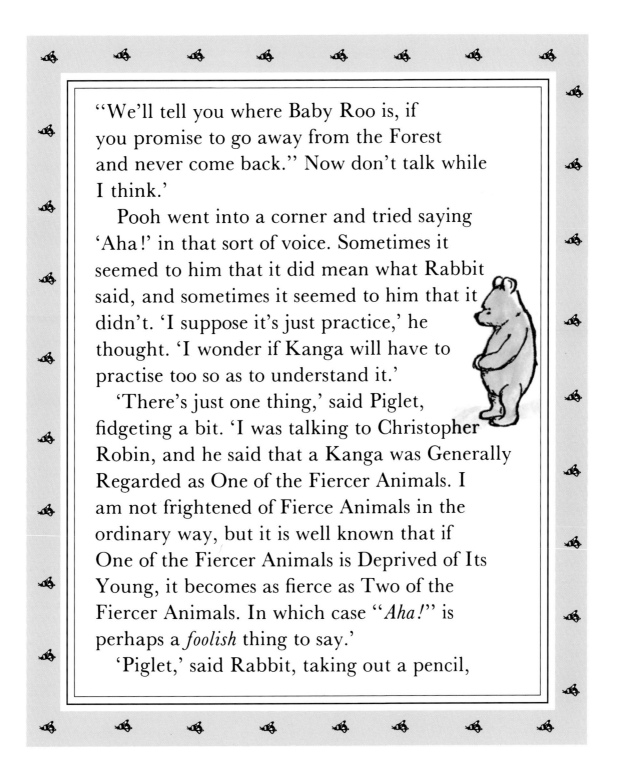

'There's just one thing,' said Piglet, fidgeting a bit. 'I was talking to Christopher Robin, and he said that a Kanga was Generally Regarded as One of the Fiercer Animals. I am not frightened of Fierce Animals in the ordinary way, but it is well known that if One of the Fiercer Animals is Deprived of Its Young, it becomes as fierce as Two of the Fiercer Animals. In which case "*Aha!*" is perhaps a *foolish* thing to say.'

'Piglet,' said Rabbit, taking out a pencil,

and licking the end of it, 'you haven't any pluck.'

'It is hard to be brave,' said Piglet, sniffing slightly, 'when you're only a Very Small Animal.'

Rabbit, who had begun to write very busily, looked up and said: 'It is because you are a very small animal that you will be Useful in the adventure before us.'

Piglet was so excited at the idea of being Useful that he forgot to be frightened any more, and when Rabbit went on to say that Kangas were only Fierce during the winter months, being at other times of an Affectionate Disposition, he could hardly sit still, he was so eager to begin being useful at once.

'What about me?' said Pooh sadly. 'I suppose *I* shan't be useful?'

'Never mind, Pooh,' said Piglet comfortingly. 'Another time perhaps.'

'Without Pooh,' said Rabbit solemnly as he sharpened his pencil, 'the adventure would be impossible.'

'Oh!' said Piglet, and tried not to look disappointed.

But Pooh went into a corner of the room and said proudly to himself, 'Impossible without Me! *That* sort of Bear.'

'Now listen all of you,' said Rabbit when he had finished writing, and Pooh and Piglet sat listening very eagerly with their mouths open. This was what Rabbit read out:

PLAN TO CAPTURE BABY ROO

1. *General Remarks.* Kanga runs faster than any of Us, even Me.
2. *More General Remarks.* Kanga never takes her eyes off Baby Roo, except when he's safely buttoned up in her pocket.

3. *Therefore.* If we are to capture Baby Roo, we must get a Long Start, because Kanga runs faster than any of Us, even Me. (*See* 1.)

4. *A Thought.* If Roo had jumped out of Kanga's pocket and Piglet had jumped in, Kanga wouldn't know the difference, because Piglet is a Very Small Animal.

5. Like Roo.

6. But Kanga would have to be looking the other way first, so as not to see Piglet jumping in.

7. See 2.

8. *Another Thought.* But if Pooh was talking to her very excitedly, she *might* look the other way for a moment.

9. And then I could run away with Roo.

10. Quickly.

11. *And Kanga wouldn't discover the difference until Afterwards.*

Well, Rabbit read this out proudly, and for a little while after he had read it nobody said anything. And then Piglet, who had been opening and shutting his mouth without making any noise, managed to say very huskily:

'And – Afterwards?'

'How do you mean?'

'When Kanga *does* Discover the Difference?'

'Then we all say "*Aha!*"'

'All three of us?'

'Yes.'

'Oh!'

'Why, what's the trouble, Piglet?'

'Nothing,' said Piglet, 'as long as *we all three* say it. As long as we all three say it,' said Piglet, 'I don't mind,' he said, 'but I shouldn't care to say "*Aha!*" by myself. It wouldn't sound *nearly* so well. By the way,' he said, 'you *are* quite sure about what you said about the winter months?'

'The winter months?'

'Yes, only being Fierce in the Winter Months.'

'Oh, yes, yes, that's all right. Well, Pooh? You see what you have to do?'

'No,' said Pooh Bear. 'Not yet,' he said. 'What *do* I do?'

'Well, you just have to talk very hard to Kanga so as she doesn't notice anything.'

'Oh! What about?'

'Anything you like.'

'You mean like telling her a little bit of poetry or something?'

'That's it,' said Rabbit. 'Splendid. Now come along.'

So they all went out to look for Kanga.

Kanga and Roo were spending a quiet afternoon in a sandy part of the Forest. Baby Roo was practising very small jumps in the sand, and falling down mouse-holes and climbing out of them, and Kanga was fidgeting about and saying 'Just one more jump, dear, and then we must go home.' And at that moment who should come stumping up the hill but Pooh.

'Good afternoon, Kanga.'

'Good afternoon, Pooh.'

'Look at me jumping,' squeaked Roo, and fell into another mouse-hole.

'Hallo, Roo, my little fellow!'

'We were just going home,' said Kanga. 'Good afternoon, Rabbit. Good afternoon, Piglet.'

Rabbit and Piglet, who had now come up from the other side of the hill, said 'Good afternoon,' and 'Hallo, Roo,' and Roo asked them to look at him jumping, so they stayed and looked.

And Kanga looked too. . . .

'Oh, Kanga,' said Pooh, after Rabbit had winked at him twice, 'I don't know if you are interested in Poetry at all?'

'Hardly at all,' said Kanga.

'Oh!' said Pooh.

'Roo, dear, just one more jump and then
we must go home.'

There was a short silence while Roo fell
down another mouse-hole.

'Go on,' said Rabbit in a loud whisper
behind his paw.

'Talking of Poetry,' said Pooh, 'I made up
a little piece as I was coming along. It went like
this. Er – now let me see—'

'Fancy!' said Kanga. 'Now Roo, dear—'

'You'll like this piece of poetry,' said Rabbit.

'You'll love it,' said Piglet.

'You must listen very carefully,' said Rabbit.

'So as not to miss any of it,' said Piglet.

'Oh, yes,' said Kanga, but she still looked at Baby Roo.

'*How* did it go, Pooh?' said Rabbit.

Pooh gave a little cough and began.

LINES WRITTEN BY
A BEAR OF VERY LITTLE BRAIN

On Monday, when the sun is hot
I wonder to myself a lot:
'Now is it true, or is it not,
'That what is which and which is what?'

On Tuesday, when it hails and snows,
The feeling on me grows and grows
That hardly anybody knows
If those are these or these are those.

On Wednesday, when the sky is blue,
And I have nothing else to do,
I sometimes wonder if it's true
That who is what and what is who.

On Thursday, when it starts to freeze
And hoar-frost twinkles on the trees,
How very readily one sees
That these are whose – but whose are these?

On Friday—

'Yes, it is, isn't it?' said Kanga, not waiting to hear what happened on Friday. 'Just one more jump, Roo, dear, and then we really *must* be going.'

Rabbit gave Pooh a hurrying-up sort of nudge.

'Talking of Poetry,' said Pooh quickly, 'have you ever noticed that tree right over there?'

'Where?' said Kanga. 'Now, Roo—'

'Right over there,' said Pooh, pointing behind Kanga's back.

'No,' said Kanga. 'Now jump in, Roo, dear, and we'll go home.'

'You ought to look at that tree right over there,' said Rabbit. 'Shall I lift you in, Roo?' And he picked up Roo in his paws.

'I can see a bird in it from here,' said Pooh. 'Or is it a fish?'

'You ought to see that bird from here,' said Rabbit. 'Unless it's a fish.'

'It isn't a fish, it's a bird,' said Piglet.

'So it is,' said Rabbit.

'Is it a starling or a blackbird?' said Pooh.

'That's the whole question,' said Rabbit. 'Is it a blackbird or a starling?'

And then at last Kanga did turn her head to look. And the moment that her head was turned, Rabbit said in a loud voice 'In you go, Roo!' and in jumped Piglet into Kanga's pocket, and off scampered Rabbit, with Roo in his paws, as fast as he could.

'Why, where's Rabbit?' said Kanga, turning round again. 'Are you all right, Roo, dear?'

Piglet made a squeaky Roo-noise from the bottom of Kanga's pocket.

'Rabbit had to go away,' said Pooh. 'I think he thought of something he had to go and see about suddenly.'

'And Piglet?'

'I think Piglet thought of something at the same time. Suddenly.'

'Well, we must be getting home,' said

Kanga. 'Good-bye, Pooh.' And in three large jumps she was gone.

Pooh looked after her as she went.

'I wish I could jump like that,' he thought. 'Some can and some can't. That's how it is.'

But there were moments when Piglet wished that Kanga couldn't. Often, when he had had a long walk home through the Forest, he had wished that he were a bird; but now he thought jerkily to himself at the bottom of Kanga's pocket,

this   take

'If   is   shall   really   to

       flying I   never   it.'

And as he went up in the air he said, '*Ooooooo!*' and as he came down he said, '*Ow!*' And he was saying, '*Ooooooo-ow, Ooooooo-ow, Ooooooo-ow*' all the way to Kanga's house.

Of course as soon as Kanga unbuttoned her pocket, she saw what had happened. Just for a moment, she thought she was frightened, and then she knew she wasn't; for she felt sure that Christopher Robin would never let any harm happen to Roo. So she said to herself, 'If they are having a joke with me, I will have a joke with them.'

'Now then, Roo, dear,' she said as she took Piglet out of her pocket. 'Bed-time.'

'*Aha!*' said Piglet, as well as he could after his Terrifying Journey. But it wasn't

a very good '*Aha!*' and Kanga didn't seem
to understand what it meant.

'Bath first,' said Kanga in a cheerful
voice.

'*Aha!*' said Piglet again, looking anxiously
for the others. But the others weren't there.
Rabbit was playing with Baby Roo in his own
house, and feeling more fond of him every
minute, and Pooh, who had decided to be
a Kanga, was still at the sandy place on the top
of the Forest, practising jumps.

'I am not at all sure,' said Kanga in a
thoughtful voice, 'that it wouldn't be
a good idea to have a *cold* bath this
evening. Would you like that, Roo, dear?'

Piglet, who had never been really fond
of baths, shuddered a long indignant
shudder, and said in as brave a voice as
he could: 'Kanga, I see that the time has
come to speak plainly.'

'Funny little Roo,' said Kanga, as she
got the bath-water ready.

'I am *not* Roo,' said Piglet loudly. 'I
am Piglet!'

'Yes, dear, yes,' said Kanga soothingly.
'And imitating Piglet's voice too! So
clever of him,' she went on, as she took

a large bar of yellow soap out of the cupboard. 'What *will* he be doing next?'

'Can't you *see*?' shouted Piglet. 'Haven't you got *eyes*? *Look* at me!'

'I *am* looking, Roo, dear,' said Kanga rather severely. 'And you know what I told you yesterday about making faces. If you go on making faces like Piglet's you will grow up to *look* like Piglet – and *then* think how sorry you will be. Now then, into the bath, and don't let me have to speak to you about it again.'

Before he knew where he was, Piglet was in the bath, and Kanga was scrubbing him firmly with a large lathery flannel.

'*Ow!*' cried Piglet. 'Let me out! I'm Piglet!'

'Don't open the mouth, dear, or the soap goes in,' said Kanga. 'There! What did I tell you?'

'You – you – you did it on purpose,' spluttered Piglet, as soon as he could speak again . . . and then accidentally had another mouthful of lathery flannel.

'That's right, dear, don't say anything,' said Kanga, and in another minute Piglet was out of the bath, and being rubbed dry with a towel.

'Now,' said Kanga, 'there's your medicine, and then bed.'

'W-w-what medicine?' said Piglet.

'To make you grow big and strong, dear. You don't want to grow up small and weak

like Piglet, do you? Well, then!'

At that moment there was a knock at the door.

'Come in,' said Kanga, and in came Christopher Robin.

'Christopher Robin, Christopher Robin!' cried Piglet. 'Tell Kanga who I am! She keeps saying I'm Roo. I'm not Roo, am I!'

Christopher Robin looked at him very carefully, and shook his head.

'You can't be Roo,' he said, 'because I've just seen Roo playing in Rabbit's house.'

'Well!' said Kanga. 'Fancy that! Fancy my making a mistake like that.'

'There you are!' said Piglet. 'I told you so. I'm Piglet.'

Christopher Robin shook his head again.

'Oh, you're not Piglet,' he said. 'I know Piglet well, and he's *quite* a different colour.'

Piglet began to say that this was because he had just had a bath, and then he thought that perhaps he wouldn't say that, and as he opened his mouth to say something else, Kanga slipped the medicine spoon in, and then patted him on the back and told him that it was really quite a nice taste when you got used to it.

'I knew it wasn't Piglet,' said Kanga. 'I wonder who it can be.'

'Perhaps it's some relation of Pooh's,' said Christopher Robin. 'What about a nephew or an uncle or something?'

Kanga agreed that this was probably what it was, and said that they would have to call it by some name.

'I shall call it Pootel,' said Christopher Robin. 'Henry Pootel for short.'

And just when it was decided, Henry Pootel wriggled out of Kanga's arms and jumped to the ground. To his great joy Christopher Robin had left the door open. Never had Henry Pootel Piglet run so fast as he ran then, and he didn't stop running until he had got quite close to his house. But when he was a hundred yards away he stopped running, and rolled the rest of the way home, so as to get his own nice comfortable colour again. . . .

So Kanga and Roo stayed in the Forest. And every Tuesday Roo spent the day with his great friend Rabbit, and every Tuesday Kanga spent the day with her great friend Pooh, teaching him to jump, and every Tuesday Piglet spent the day with his great friend Christopher Robin. So they were all happy again.

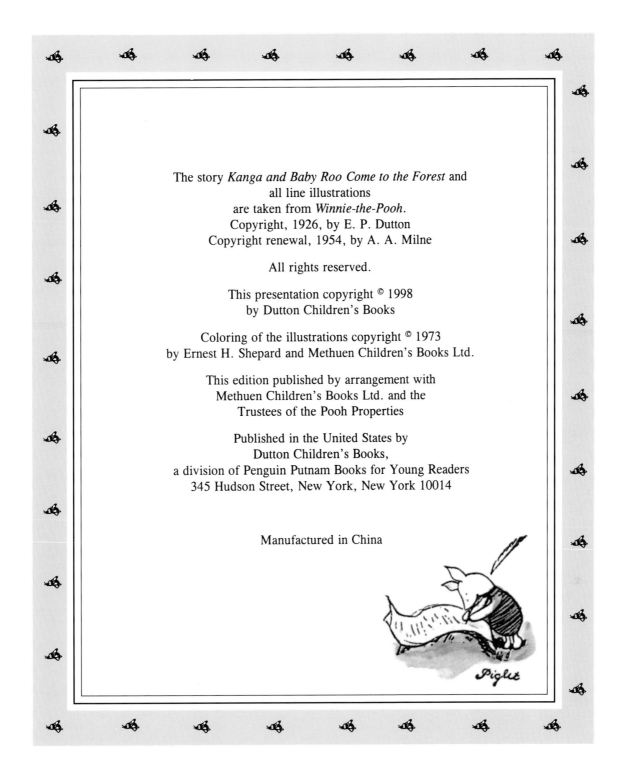

A. A. MILNE

Tigger Comes to the Forest and Has Breakfast

illustrated by
E. H. SHEPARD

DUTTON CHILDREN'S BOOKS

Tigger Comes to the Forest
and Has Breakfast

Winnie-the-Pooh woke up suddenly in the middle of the night and listened. Then he got out of bed, and lit his candle, and stumped across the room to see if anybody was trying to get into his honey-cupboard, and they weren't, so he stumped back again, blew out his candle, and got into bed. Then he heard the noise again.

'Is that you, Piglet?' he said.

But it wasn't.

'Come in, Christopher Robin,' he said.

But Christopher Robin didn't.

'Tell me about it to-morrow, Eeyore,' said Pooh sleepily.

But the noise went on.

'*Worraworraworraworraworra*,' said Whatever-it-was, and Pooh found that he wasn't asleep after all.

'What can it be?' he thought. 'There are lots of noises in the Forest, but this is a different one. It isn't a growl, and it isn't a purr, and it isn't a bark, and it isn't the noise-you-make-before-beginning-a-piece-of-poetry, but it's a noise of some kind, made by a strange animal! And he's making it outside my door. So I shall get up and ask him not to do it.'

He got out of bed and opened his front door.

'Hallo!' said Pooh, in case there was anything outside.

'Hallo!' said Whatever-it-was.

'Oh!' said Pooh. 'Hallo!'

'Hallo!'

'Oh, *there* you are!' said Pooh. 'Hallo!'

'Hallo!' said the Strange Animal, wondering how long this was going on.

Pooh was just going to say 'Hallo!' for the fourth time when he thought that he

wouldn't, so he said, 'Who is it?' instead.

'Me,' said a voice.

'Oh!' said Pooh. 'Well, come here.'

So Whatever-it-was came here, and in the light of the candle he and Pooh looked at each other.

'I'm Pooh,' said Pooh.

'I'm Tigger,' said Tigger.

'Oh!' said Pooh, for he had never seen an animal like this before. 'Does Christopher Robin know about you?'

'Of course he does,' said Tigger.

'Well,' said Pooh, 'it's the middle of the night, which is a good time for going to sleep. And to-morrow morning we'll have some honey for breakfast. Do Tiggers like honey?'

'They like everything,' said Tigger cheerfully.

'Then if they like going to sleep on the floor, I'll go back to bed,' said Pooh, 'and we'll do things in the morning. Good Night.'

And he got back into bed and went fast asleep.

When he awoke in the morning, the first thing he saw was Tigger, sitting in front of the glass and looking at himself.

'Hallo!' said Pooh.

'Hallo!' said Tigger. 'I've found

somebody just like me. I thought I was the only one of them.'

Pooh got out of bed, and began to explain what a looking-glass was, but just as he was getting to the interesting part, Tigger said:

'Excuse me a moment, but there's something climbing up your table,' and with one loud *Worraworraworraworraworra* he jumped at the end of the tablecloth, pulled it to the ground, wrapped himself up in it three times, rolled to the other end of the room, and, after a terrible struggle, got his head into the daylight again, and said cheerfully: 'Have I won?'

'That's my tablecloth,' said Pooh, as he began to unwind Tigger.

'I wondered what it was,' said Tigger.

'It goes on the table and you put things on it.'

'Then why did it try to bite me when I wasn't looking?'

'I don't *think* it did,' said Pooh.

'It tried,' said Tigger, 'but I was too quick for it.'

Pooh put the cloth back on the table, and he put a large honey-pot on the cloth, and they sat down to breakfast. And as soon as they sat down, Tigger took a large mouthful

of honey . . . and he looked up at the ceiling with his head on one side, and made exploring

noises with his tongue, and considering
noises, and what-have-we-got-*here* noises . .
and then he said in a very decided voice:

'Tiggers don't like honey.'

'Oh!' said Pooh, and tried to make it sound
Sad and Regretful. 'I thought they liked
everything.'

'Everything except honey,' said Tigger.

Pooh felt rather pleased about this, and
said that, as soon as he had finished his
own breakfast, he would take Tigger round to
Piglet's house, and Tigger could try some of
Piglet's haycorns.

'Thank you, Pooh,' said Tigger, 'because
haycorns is really what Tiggers like best.'

So after breakfast they went round to
see Piglet, and Pooh explained as they went
that Piglet was a Very Small Animal who
didn't like bouncing, and asked Tigger not to
be too Bouncy just at first. And Tigger,
who had been hiding behind trees and jumping
out on Pooh's shadow when it wasn't looking,

said that Tiggers were only bouncy before
breakfast, and that as soon as they had had
a few haycorns they became Quiet and Refined.
So by-and-by they knocked at the door of
Piglet's house.

'Hallo, Pooh,' said Piglet.

'Hallo, Piglet. This is Tigger.'

'Oh, is it?' said Piglet, and he edged
round to the other side of the table. 'I
thought Tiggers were smaller than that.'

'Not the big ones,' said Tigger.

'They like haycorns,' said Pooh, 'so that's what we've come for, because poor Tigger hasn't had any breakfast yet.'

Piglet pushed the bowl of haycorns towards Tigger, and said, 'Help yourself,' and then he got close up to Pooh and felt

much braver, and said, 'So you're Tigger? Well, well!' in a careless sort of voice. But Tigger said nothing because his mouth was full of haycorns. . . .

After a long munching noise he said:
'Ee-ers o i a-ors.'

And when Pooh and Piglet said 'What?'
he said 'Skoos ee,' and went outside for
a moment.

When he came back he said firmly:
'Tiggers don't like haycorns.'

'But you said they liked everything except
honey,' said Pooh.

'Everything except honey *and* haycorns,'
explained Tigger.

When he heard this, Pooh said, 'Oh, I
see!' and Piglet, who was rather glad that
Tiggers didn't like haycorns, said, 'What
about thistles?'

'Thistles,' said Tigger, 'is what Tiggers
like best.'

'Then let's go along and see Eeyore,'
said Piglet.

So the three of them went; and after they
had walked and walked and walked, they came
to the part of the Forest where Eeyore was.

'Hallo, Eeyore!' said Pooh. 'This is Tigger.'

'What is?' said Eeyore.

'This,' explained Pooh and Piglet together, and Tigger smiled his happiest smile and said nothing.

Eeyore walked all round Tigger one way, and then turned and walked all round him the other way.

'What did you say it was?' he asked.

'Tigger.'

'Ah!' said Eeyore.

'He's just come,' explained Piglet.

'Ah!' said Eeyore again.

He thought for a long time and then said:

'When is he going?'

Pooh explained to Eeyore that Tigger was a great friend of Christopher Robin's, who had come to stay in the Forest, and Piglet explained to Tigger that he mustn't mind what Eeyore said because he was *always* gloomy; and Eeyore explained to Piglet that,

on the contrary, he was feeling particularly cheerful this morning; and Tigger explained to anybody who was listening that he hadn't had any breakfast yet.

'I knew there was something,' said Pooh. 'Tiggers always eat thistles, so that was why we came to see you, Eeyore.'

'Don't mention it, Pooh.'

'Oh, Eeyore, I didn't mean that I didn't *want* to see you—'

'Quite – quite. But your new stripy friend – naturally, he wants his breakfast. What did you say his name was?'

'Tigger.'

'Then come this way, Tigger.'

Eeyore led the way to the most thistly-looking patch of thistles that ever was, and waved a hoof at it.

'A little patch I was keeping for my birthday,' he said; 'but, after all, what *are* birthdays? Here to-day and gone to-morrow. Help yourself, Tigger.'

Tigger thanked him and looked a little anxiously at Pooh.

'Are these really thistles?' he whispered.

'Yes,' said Pooh.

'What Tiggers like best?'

'That's right,' said Pooh.

'I see,' said Tigger.

So he took a large mouthful, and he gave a large crunch.

'*Ow!*' said Tigger.

He sat down and put his paw in his mouth.

'What's the matter?' asked Pooh.

'*Hot!*' mumbled Tigger.

'Your friend,' said Eeyore, 'appears to have bitten on a bee.'

Pooh's friend stopped shaking his head to get the prickles out, and explained that Tiggers didn't like thistles.

'Then why bend a perfectly good one?' asked Eeyore.

'But you said,' began Pooh, '—you *said* that Tiggers liked everything except honey and haycorns.'

'*And* thistles,' said Tigger, who was now running round in circles with his tongue hanging out.

Pooh looked at him sadly.

'What are we going to do?' he asked Piglet.

Piglet knew the answer to that, and he said at once that they must go and see Christopher Robin.

'You'll find him with Kanga,' said Eeyore.

He came close to Pooh, and said in
a loud whisper:

'*Could* you ask your friend to do his
exercises somewhere else? I shall be
having lunch directly, and don't want it
bounced on just before I begin. A trifling
matter, and fussy of me, but we all have our
little ways.'

Pooh nodded solemnly and called to Tigger.

'Come along and we'll go and see Kanga.
She's sure to have lots of breakfast for you.'

Tigger finished his last circle and came
up to Pooh and Piglet.

'Hot!' he explained with a large and friendly smile. 'Come on!' and he rushed off.

Pooh and Piglet walked slowly after him. And as they walked Piglet said nothing because he couldn't think of anything, and Pooh said nothing, because he was thinking of a poem. And when he had thought of it he began:

What shall we do about poor little Tigger?
If he never eats nothing he'll never get bigger.
He doesn't like honey and haycorns and thistles
Because of the taste and because of the bristles.
And all the good things which an animal likes
Have the wrong sort of swallow or too many
      spikes.

'He's quite big enough anyhow,' said Piglet.

'He isn't *really* very big.'

'Well, he *seems* so.'

Pooh was thoughtful when he heard this,
and then he murmured to himself:

> But whatever his weight in pounds,
>   shillings, and ounces,
> He always seems bigger because
>   of his bounces.

'And that's the whole poem,' he said.
'Do you like it, Piglet?'
'All except the shillings,' said Piglet.
'I don't think they ought to be there.'

'They wanted to come in after the pounds,' explained Pooh, 'so I let them. It is the best way to write poetry, letting things come.'

'Oh, I didn't know,' said Piglet.

Tigger had been bouncing in front of them all this time, turning round every now and then to ask, 'Is this the way?' – and now at last they came in sight of Kanga's house, and there was Christopher Robin. Tigger rushed up to him.

'Oh, there you are, Tigger!' said Christopher Robin. 'I knew you'd be somewhere.'

'I've been finding things in the Forest,' said Tigger importantly. 'I've found a pooh and a piglet and an eeyore, but I can't find any breakfast.'

Pooh and Piglet came up and hugged Christopher Robin, and explained what had been happening.

'Don't *you* know what Tiggers like?' asked Pooh.

'I expect if I thought very hard I should,'

said Christopher Robin, 'but I *thought* Tigger knew.'

'I do,' said Tigger. 'Everything there is in the world except honey and haycorns and – what were those hot things called?'

'Thistles.'

'Yes, and those.'

'Oh, well then, Kanga can give you some breakfast.'

So they went into Kanga's house, and when Roo had said, 'Hallo, Pooh,' and 'Hallo, Piglet' once, and 'Hallo, Tigger' twice, because he had never said it before and it sounded funny, they told Kanga what they wanted, and Kanga said very kindly, 'Well, look in my cupboard, Tigger dear, and see what you'd like.' Because she knew at once that, however big Tigger seemed to be, he wanted as much kindness as Roo.

'Shall I look, too?' said Pooh, who was

beginning to feel a little eleven o'clockish. And he found a small tin of condensed milk, and something seemed to tell him

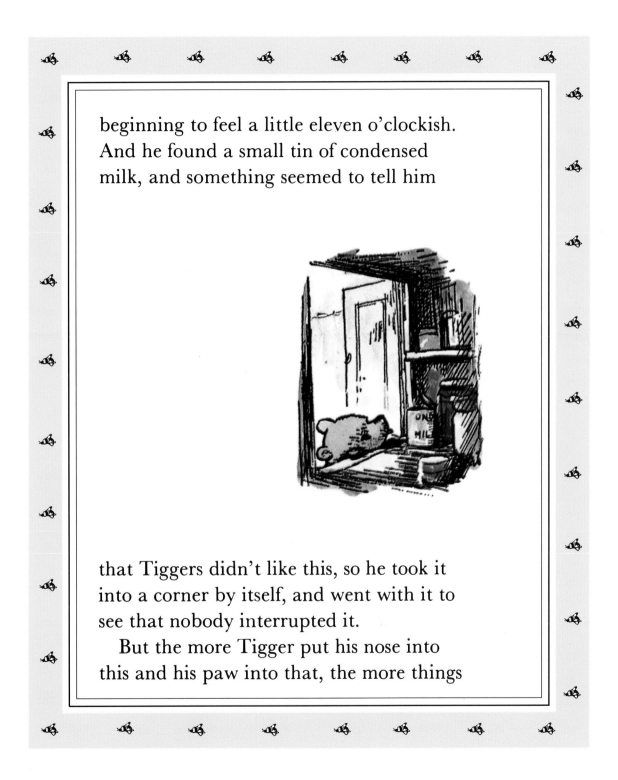

that Tiggers didn't like this, so he took it into a corner by itself, and went with it to see that nobody interrupted it.

But the more Tigger put his nose into this and his paw into that, the more things

he found which Tiggers didn't like. And when
he had found everything in the cupboard,
and couldn't eat any of it, he said to
Kanga, 'What happens now?'

But Kanga and Christopher Robin and
Piglet were all standing round Roo, watching
him have his Extract of Malt. And Roo
was saying, 'Must I?' and Kanga was saying,
'Now, Roo dear, you remember what you
promised.'

'What is it?' whispered Tigger to
Piglet.

'His Strengthening Medicine,' said Piglet.
'He hates it.'

So Tigger came closer, and he leant over
the back of Roo's chair, and suddenly he
put out his tongue, and took one large
golollop, and, with a sudden jump of surprise,

Kanga said, 'Oh!' and then clutched at the
spoon again, just as it was disappearing, and
pulled it safely back out of Tigger's mouth.
But the Extract of Malt had gone.

'Tigger *dear*!' said Kanga.

'He's taken my medicine, he's taken my
medicine, he's taken my medicine!' said Roo
happily, thinking it was a tremendous joke.

Then Tigger looked up at the ceiling, and
closed his eyes, and his tongue went round

and round his chops, in case he had left any outside, and a peaceful smile came over his face as he said, 'So *that's* what Tiggers like!'

Which explains why he always lived at Kanga's house afterwards, and had Extract of Malt for breakfast, dinner, and tea. And sometimes, when Kanga thought he wanted strengthening, he had a spoonful or two of Roo's breakfast after meals as medicine.

'But *I* think,' said Piglet to Pooh, 'that he's been strengthened quite enough.'

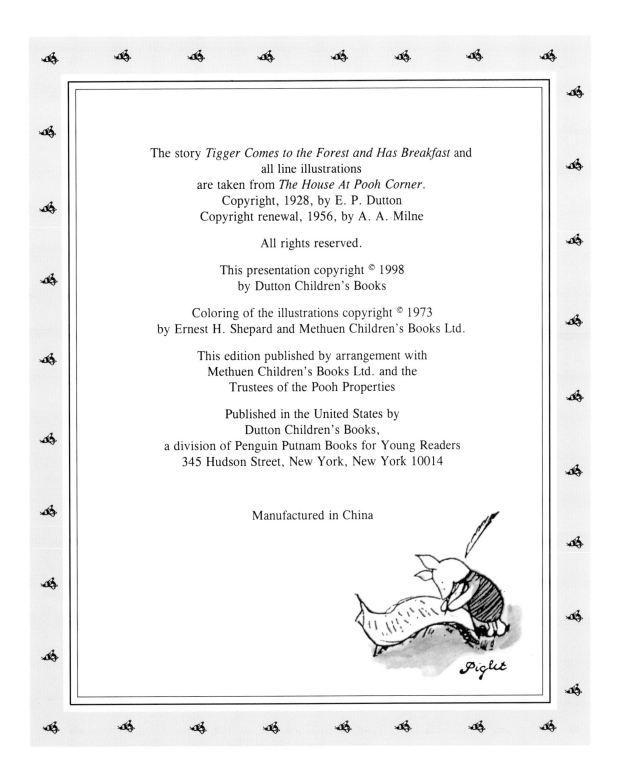